GLOBALVIEWPOINTS

The War in Iraq

Other Books of Related Interest:

At Issue Series

Does the World Hate the U.S.?

Foreign Oil Dependence

How Safe Is America's Infrastructure?

How Should the U.S. Proceed in Iraq?

National Security

Should Governments Negotiate with Terrorists?

Current Controversies Series

Domestic Wiretapping

Homeland Security

Introducing Issues with Opposing Viewpoints Series

Oil

Issues on Trial

Terrorism

Opposing Viewpoints Series

Terrorism

GLOBALVIEWPOINTS

The War in Iraq

Tom Lansford, Book Editor

GREENHAVEN PRESS
A part of Gale, Cengage Learning

GALE
CENGAGE Learning™

Detroit • New York • San Francisco • New Haven, Conn • Waterville, Maine • London

Christine Nasso, *Publisher*
Elizabeth Des Chenes, *Managing Editor*

© 2009 Greenhaven Press, a part of Gale, Cengage Learning

Gale and Greenhaven Press are registered trademarks used herein under license.

For more information, contact:
Greenhaven Press
27500 Drake Rd.
Farmington Hills, MI 48331-3535
Or you can visit our Internet site at gale.cengage.com

For product information and technology assistance, contact us at

Gale Customer Support, 1-800-877-4253
For permission to use material from this text or product, submit all requests online at www.cengage.com/permissions

Further permissions questions can be emailed to permissionrequest@cengage.com

Articles in Greenhaven Press anthologies are often edited for length to meet page requirements. In addition, original titles of these works are changed to clearly present the main thesis and to explicitly indicate the author's opinion. Every effort is made to ensure that Greenhaven Press accurately reflects the original intent of the authors. Every effort has been made to trace the owners of copyrighted material.

Cover image reproduced from Gianluigi Guercia/Getty Images.

LIBRARY OF CONGRESS CATALOGING-IN-PUBLICATION DATA

The war in Iraq / Tom Lansford, book editor.
   p. cm. -- (Global viewpoints)
   Includes bibliographical references and index.
   ISBN 978-0-7377-4162-9 (hardcover)
   ISBN 978-0-7377-4163-6 (pbk.)
   1. Iraq War, 2003-. I. Lansford, Tom.
   DS79.76.W359 2009
   956.7044'3--dc22

                2008053992

Printed in the United States of America
1 2 3 4 5 6 7 13 12 11 10 09

Contents

Chapter 2: The Iraq War and the Arab-Israeli Conflict

Chapter 3: The Iraq War and International Terrorism

Chapter 4: The Iraq War and Democracy

Foreword

> "The problems of all of humanity can
> only be solved by all of humanity."
> —Swiss author Friedrich Dürrenmatt

Global interdependence has become an undeniable reality. Mass media and technology have increased worldwide access to information and created a society of global citizens. Understanding and navigating this global community is a challenge, requiring a high degree of information literacy and a new level of learning sophistication.

Building on the success of its flagship series, *Opposing Viewpoints*, Greenhaven Press has created the *Global Viewpoints* series to examine a broad range of current, often controversial topics of worldwide importance from a variety of international perspectives. Providing students and other readers with the information they need to explore global connections and think critically about worldwide implications, each *Global Viewpoints* volume offers a panoramic view of a topic of widespread significance.

Drugs, famine, immigration—a broad, international treatment is essential to do justice to social, environmental, health, and political issues such as these. Junior high, high school, and early college students, as well as general readers, can all use *Global Viewpoints* anthologies to discern the complexities relating to each issue. Readers will be able to examine unique national perspectives while, at the same time, appreciating the interconnectedness that global priorities bring to all nations and cultures.

Material in each volume is selected from a diverse range of sources, including journals, magazines, newspapers, nonfiction books, speeches, government documents, pamphlets, organization newsletters, and position papers. *Global Viewpoints* is truly global, with material drawn primarily from international sources available in English and secondarily from U.S. sources with extensive international coverage.

Features of each volume in the *Global Viewpoints* series include:

- An **annotated table of contents** that provides a brief summary of each essay in the volume, including the name of the country or area covered in the essay.

- An **introduction** specific to the volume topic.

- A **world map** to help readers locate the countries or areas covered in the essays.

- For each viewpoint, an **introduction** that contains notes about the author and source of the viewpoint explains why material from the specific country is being presented, summarizes the main points of the viewpoint, and offers three **guided reading questions** to aid in understanding and comprehension.

- **For further discussion** questions that promote critical thinking by asking the reader to compare and contrast aspects of the viewpoints or draw conclusions about perspectives and arguments.

- A worldwide list of **organizations to contact** for readers seeking additional information.

- A **periodical bibliography** for each chapter and a **bibliography of books** on the volume topic to aid in further research.

- A comprehensive **subject index** to offer access to people, places, events, and subjects cited in the text, with the countries covered in the viewpoints highlighted.

Global Viewpoints is designed for a broad spectrum of readers who want to learn more about current events, history, political science, government, international relations, economics, environmental science, world cultures, and sociology—students doing research for class assignments or debates, teachers and faculty seeking to supplement course materials, and others wanting to understand current issues better. By presenting how people in various countries perceive the root causes, current consequences, and proposed solutions to worldwide challenges, *Global Viewpoints* volumes offer readers opportunities to enhance their global awareness and their knowledge of cultures worldwide.

Introduction

"The people of the United States and our friends and allies will not live at the mercy of an outlaw regime that threatens the peace with weapons of mass murder."

George W. Bush,
March 19, 2003

On March 20, 2003, the United States led an invasion of Iraq. The onset of the conflict came after a period of intense diplomatic interaction between nations that supported U.S. efforts to gain international approval for military action and those countries that opposed an invasion of Iraq. The conflict over whether or not to go to war created deep divisions between the United States and some of its closest allies and undermined the international standing of the nation.

In the aftermath of the September 11, 2001, terrorist attacks, the administration of George W. Bush assembled a coalition of allies to combat international terrorism and to defeat al Qaeda and its allies—the Taliban regime in Afghanistan. The subsequent invasion of Afghanistan enjoyed substantial international support, and by December 2001, most Taliban and al Qaeda fighters had been killed, had surrendered, or had fled. In a 2002 speech, Bush declared that the U.S.-led war on terror would not stop with Afghanistan. Instead Bush identified Iran, Iraq, and North Korea as part of an "axis of evil" that threatened the world through support of terrorism and efforts to acquire or proliferate weapons of mass destruction (WMD), including nuclear, biological, or chemical weapons. Bush asserted that the United States would use preemptive force to prevent another major attack on the United States like those that took place on September 11, 2001. Bush stated: "I will not wait on events, while dangers gather. . . . The United States of America will not permit the world's most dangerous regimes to threaten us with the world's most destructive weapons."

The Bush administration then initiated a diplomatic effort to gain support for strong action against Iraq, which the United States accused of sponsoring terrorism and having an ongoing program to acquire weapons of mass destruction. Some world leaders strongly supported the United States. For instance, in a speech to Parliament in April 2002, British Prime Minister Tony Blair declared that "Saddam Hussein's regime is despicable, he is developing weapons of mass destruction, and we cannot leave him doing so unchecked. He is a threat to his own people and to the region and, if allowed to develop these weapons, a threat to us also." The United Nations (UN) Security Council responded with Resolution 1441, which called upon Iraq to open itself to inspections by the UN. After the 1991 Persian Gulf War, Iraq had been subject to UN weapons inspections because of its WMD program, but in 1998 Iraq had ordered the removal of the inspectors. Meanwhile, throughout the 1990s, the United States and its allies had enforced a series of UN resolutions that imposed economic and military sanctions on Iraq. When the new round of inspections began in 2002, the United States accused Iraq of continued deception and noncompliance.

The Bush administration and its closest allies, including Australia, the United Kingdom, and Spain, began advocating for stronger action against Iraq and a second UN resolution that would authorize the use of force against the Iraqi regime of Saddam Hussein if it did not cooperate more fully with the inspections program. However, many in the UN argued that the weapons inspectors needed more time. Even close U.S. allies such as Germany and France opposed what they perceived to be a rush to war. France and Russia, permanent members of the Security Council, threatened to veto any further action on Iraq until the inspectors had completed their work. In October 2002, the U.S. Congress voted overwhelmingly to allow Bush to use force against Iraq. The vote was 77-23 in favor in the Senate, and 291-133 in the House of Representatives.

By the spring of 2003, the UN inspectors had found only minor violations of UN resolutions, including a dozen chemical weapons warheads dating back to the 1991 Gulf War and missiles that exceeded the allowable range under UN guidelines. Efforts to gain a second resolution failed and the United States shifted its focus to building a coalition of allies to aid any potential military strikes. However, key allies such as Turkey, which under military plans would have been the base of a northern invasion by U.S.-led forces, continued to oppose military action. Turkey subsequently refused to allow the United States to use its soil to launch the invasion. In the United States and abroad, there were large protests against military strikes, but polling showed that as much as 65 percent of the American public supported the war. The majority of people in some allied countries, including Australia, Canada, and the United Kingdom, supported war, but only if the UN authorized it.

Members of the Bush administration argued that the United States did not need a second UN resolution since Saddam had already violated Resolution 1441 by not fully cooperating with inspectors. On March 18, 2003, Bush issued an ultimatum to Saddam to leave Iraq within twenty-four hours. When Saddam refused, Bush authorized military strikes on March 20. The invading force consisted of American, Australian, British, and Polish troops. The U.S.-led coalition quickly overran the Iraqi defenders and captured Baghdad in April. On May 2, 2003, from the deck of an aircraft carrier, Bush announced the end of major combat operations. However, the war had only just begun, as a large insurgency spread throughout Iraq, and a long occupation of that country took hold.

More U.S. service members have died during the occupation phase of the war than during the initial combat missions. During the invasion, 138 U.S. service men and women were killed, but by the fall of 2008, more than 4,100 troops had died. The insurgency was the result of continued fighting against the coalition by Saddam loyalists and allied foreign fighters, and rising ethnic tension in Iraq between the country's three largest groups, the Shiites, Sunnis, and Kurds. Saddam was captured on December 13, 2003, and later tried and executed by an Iraqi court.

New postwar inspections were unable to find evidence of any Iraqi WMD program. This development significantly undermined America's international reputation. Public support for the war, both in the United States and abroad, quickly eroded. Meanwhile, terrorist groups such as al Qaeda have sent resources and fighters to Iraq where they could directly attack American targets. Anger in the Arab world over the U.S.-led invasion heightened anti-American, and anti-Western, sentiment. French President Jacques Chirac stated in a 2004 interview: "To a certain extent, Saddam Hussein's departure was a positive thing—but it also provoked reaction such as the mobilization in a number of countries of men and women of Islam, which has made the world more dangerous."

The Iraq War remains a contentious issue around the world. It had a significant impact on the approval rating of leaders such as Bush, Blair, and Australian Prime Minister John Howard. It also negatively impacted the ability of the United States to pursue effectively the war on terrorism. Furthermore, the war became a prominent issue in the 2008 presidential election in the United States. The viewpoints in this collection examine a range of controversies surrounding the Iraq War and its impact on international relations. The authors explore four main points: the impact of the war on international relations; its relationship to the Arab-Israeli conflict; its role in the war against terrorism; and how the Iraq

War has affected efforts to spread democracy. Even after American troops have withdrawn from Iraq, the conflict will continue to shape global politics for years to follow.

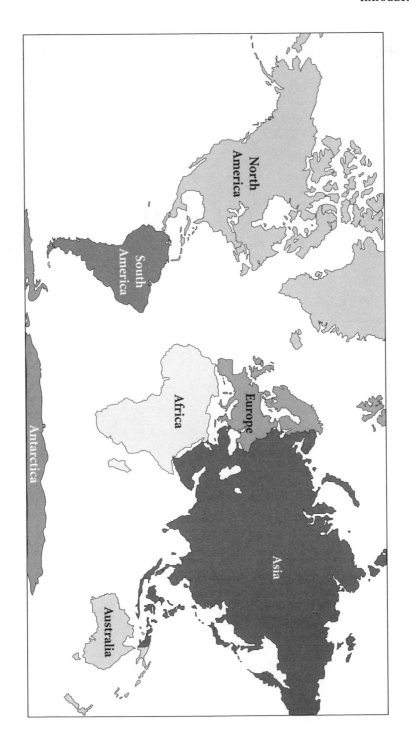

GLOBALVIEWPOINTS

CHAPTER 1

The Iraq War and International Relations

France Opposed the U.S.-Led Invasion Because of a Special Relationship Between Paris and Baghdad

Amir Taheri

In the following viewpoint written several months prior to the invasion of Iraq by U.S.-led coalition forces, author Amir Taheri argues that French opposition to the invasion was based on long-standing ties between the two countries. The viewpoint highlights the relationship between French President Jacques Chirac and Iraqi leader Saddam Hussein and the economic links between France and Iraq. The viewpoint also analyzes the efforts by the French government to develop an alternative approach to Iraq that would not involve armed conflict. Amir Taheri is the editor of a French political journal, Politique Internationale (International Politics).

As you read, consider the following questions:

1. When did President Chirac first meet Saddam Hussein?

2. What prevented Chirac from pursuing his own Iraq policy during the first five years of his presidency, according to the viewpoint?

3. According to Taheri, who did the French suggest would be a good alternative to Saddam as prime minister?

Amir Taheri, "The Chirac Doctrine: France's Iraq War Plan," *National Review Online*, November 4, 2002. www.nationalreview.com. Reproduced by permission.

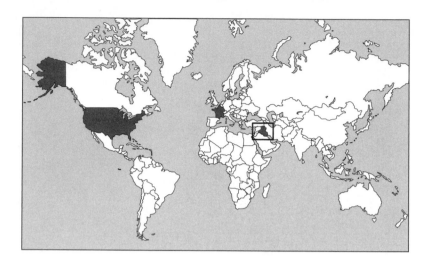

France's President Jacques Chirac is "determined" to prevent the United States from removing the Iraqi regime of President Saddam Hussein by force.

Sources in Paris insist that Chirac has decided to use the French veto in the United Nations [U.N.] Security Council, if necessary, to derail American plans for an attack on Iraq.

"If you ask me what will happen next I can tell you there will be no war," a senior French official told me on condition of anonymity. "President Chirac has taken personal charge of the Iraq dossier with the clear aim of preventing an unnecessary war that could destabilize the whole of the Middle East."

French Foreign Minister Dominique de Villepin says the status quo in Iraq is "unsustainable." But he insists that the use of force is not the only means of changing it.

French Plans

On the basis of interviews with various sources in Paris, it looks as if the French leader's plan is devised in two phases.

The first phase consists of efforts to prevent the passage of a Security Council resolution that would give the U.S. a legal basis for removing Saddam Hussein from power.

Chirac wants the U.N. weapons inspectors to return to Iraq and operate within a timeframe determined by themselves, not Washington.

French official sources believe that if there is no Iraq war within the next 10–16 weeks [late 2002–early 2003] there will be none for another two years, at least.

Hans Blix, the Swedish diplomat who heads the team of inspectors, says he may need up to 18 months before he could report to the Security Council.

Assuming that the inspectors are in Iraq by Christmas, the Blix timetable would take us into the summer of 2004. Even if he reports at that time that the Iraqis have not cooperated with his team, the issue would have to be raised by the Security Council so that a new resolution, authorizing the use of force, is discussed.

By then we would be right in the middle of the American presidential election.

French official sources believe that if there is no Iraq war within the next 10–16 weeks [late 2002–early 2003] there will be none for another two years, at least.

If President George W. Bush is reelected in 2004 he may well have less of an incentive to act against Saddam Hussein. If, on the other hand, he loses to a Democrat candidate, the new U.S. president might not want to adopt one of the Republican's most controversial policies immediately.

All but one of the likely Democratic presidential candidates have already said they are opposed to war without the full backing of the Security Council.

The second phase of Chirac's strategy consists of efforts inside Iraq to persuade Saddam to change certain aspects of his domestic and foreign policies.

"The Americans want regime change in Baghdad," says a senior French source. "But should this mean a change of personnel only? What if we could bring about significant policy changes without installing a totally new leadership that might or might not be acceptable to the Iraqi people?"

The source adds: "Chirac is convinced that he can persuade Saddam to talk the right talk and walk the right walk."

Chirac and Saddam

Chirac is the only Western leader to have a personal knowledge of the Iraqi president.

The two first met in 1975, when Chirac was prime minister for the first time, and almost instantly warmed up to one another.

Chirac became the first French leader to make an official visit to Baghdad that year, and to deepen his ties with Saddam, who was vice president and "strongman" at the time.

Saddam showed his appreciation by approving a deal under which Iraq committed to granting French oil companies a number of privileges plus a 23 percent share of Iraqi oil.

France sold an estimated $20 billion worth of weapons . . . to Iraq, and emerged as Iraq's biggest trading partner, in a wide-range of civilian goods and services, after Russia.

Chirac repaid the favor by approving the construction of Iraq's first nuclear-power center, Tammuz, near Baghdad. The project, which subsequently emerged as the core of Iraq's efforts to develop nuclear weapons, was destroyed in an Israeli air raid in September 1980.

In 1976 Saddam paid an official visit to France, his first and last to any Western country, and was received by Chirac as a head of state.

It was not until 1991 that Chirac broke contacts with Saddam as a result of Iraq's invasion of Kuwait.

Chirac's Opposition Is Not Based on Oil

A mix of motives—from boosting France's stature in the European Union and overseas to fear of a potential backlash by some 5 million Muslims living in France—may play into Chirac's pro-peace calculations. However, few believe that long-standing French oil interests in Iraq play much of a role.

"If the French were really interested in oil, they would go along with the Americans," said Guillaume Parmentier, director of the French Center on the United States, in Paris. "We know where this war is going to go. The Americans are going to win."

Elizabeth Bryant, "France Says 'Oui' to Chirac's 'Non' on Iraq War,"
San Francisco Chronicle, *February 22, 2003. www.sfgate.com.*

The friendship forged between the two men proved profitable for both sides. France sold an estimated $20 billion worth of weapons, including Mirage fighters, to Iraq, and emerged as Iraq's biggest trading partner, in a wide-range of civilian goods and services, after Russia. In exchange, Iraq focused on France as its largest oil market in Europe.

Chirac's Iraq Policy

During five of his seven-year first term as president, Chirac was unable to pursue an Iraq policy of his own because he had to contend with a Socialist-Communist cabinet headed by his then political rival Lionel Jospin.

Since last April [2002], however, Chirac, with his supporters in control of both the parliament and the cabinet, has assumed personal charge of the Iraqi issue by setting up a special "policy cell" within the Elysee Palace. Chirac has dispatched a special emissary to Baghdad to sound out "the possibility of change without war."

The emissary is Pierre Delval, described by many as a brilliant young diplomat.

He first went to Baghdad using as cover the post of director of the French state-owned National Printing Company, but has since been seconded to the Quai d'Orsay, the French foreign office.

The Delval mission is designed in a way as to allow him to spend ten days in Iraq each month, thus giving Paris a direct diplomatic presence in the absence of an ambassador.

According to sources, Iraqi response to Delval has been "more than encouraging."

This was symbolized by the fact that Saddam Hussein invited the French diplomat to attend a four-hour session of the Iraqi government last month [October 2002] when the latest threats from Washington were debated.

Delval's main Iraqi contact man is Tareq Aziz, the veteran Baathist leader who has been close to the French for years.

In recent months, however, Delval has also forged links with Qussai, Saddam Hussein's younger son. The two have met on at least six occasions and held "very broad discussions on all aspects of policy."

French sources believe that Qussai, unlike his elder brother Uday whom they describe as "unpredictable," could play a central role in a period of transition.

One idea is for Qussai to be appointed prime minister, a post now held by Saddam himself, so that he can form a cabinet of new generation and bring in new faces, mostly technocrats.

Another French idea is that the Baath party, now controlled by Uday, should be revived under a new leadership.

Delval has met several Baath leaders to evoke the possibility of a congress in which the Iraqi ruling party could "carry out major reforms of policy and personnel."

The French believe that the Baath remains a real political force in Iraq and should not be dismissed out of hand.

Paris sources claim that Saddam's decision to announce a general amnesty, including the release of all political prisoners, is a response to French suggestions.

Another French suggestion is that Saddam should announce an amnesty, perhaps next April [2003], for Iraqis in exile, inviting them all to return home and help rebuild the country.

Another part of the plan is to hold fresh parliamentary elections, perhaps next autumn, so that a more credible legislature could be formed. The French want the new parliament to include members from the two principal Kurdish parties plus the Iraqi Communist party, and independents, especially women.

French Support for the Saddam Regime

Unlike Washington that presents Iraq's leadership as a coterie of war criminals, Paris insists that the Iraqi ruling elite includes many "valuable individuals."

One senior French official even told us that Paris believed that Iraq had "potentially the most effective leadership group in the whole of the Arab world."

Apart from Qussai and Tareq Aziz, Iraqi officials who appear to be supporting the French initiative include the National Assembly Speaker Saadoun Hammadi, diplomatic advisor Nizar Hamdoun, Commerce Minister Muhamamd Mahdi-Saleh, head of the Central Bank Muhammad al-Hawwash, presidential adviser Abdulrazzaq al-Hashemi, Industry Minister Amer al-Rashid, and Foreign Minister Naji al-Sabri.

To these are added a number of technocrats, senior civil servants, university teachers, and private businessmen with links to France.

"We can change Iraq without war," says a French source. "All we need is time to show that our scenario works better than that of Washington."

What France is proposing in Iraq is already seen in Paris as "the Chirac Doctrine" which is aimed at persuading "trouble-making regimes" to accept peaceful change.

The question is: Will Washington stand back and watch while the Chirac doctrine is put to its first major test?

Iran Has Expanded Its Influence in the Middle East as a Result of the Iraq War

Suzanne Maloney

In the following viewpoint, Suzanne Maloney examines Iran's efforts to increase its power and influence in the region in the midst of the Iraq War. Maloney contends that while the administration of George W. Bush believed before the invasion that Iraq would serve as a counterweight to Iran, instead the Iranian government has developed a significant degree of sway in the Middle East. In addition, other states in the region, including key U.S. allies, are increasingly cooperative with Iran. Maloney is a former official at the U.S. State Department and currently focuses on Iran and the Middle East as a senior fellow at the Brookings Institution.

As you read, consider the following questions:

1. Who was the first regional leader to visit Iraq after the 2003 U.S.-led invasion?

2. According to the viewpoint, why has Iran supported insurgents in Iraq?

3. What does the viewpoint cite as examples of initiatives that the United States used to "capitalize" on Sunni Arab opposition to Iran?

Suzanne Maloney, "How the Iraq War Has Empowered Iran," March 21, 2008. www.brookings.edu. © 2008 The Brookings Institution. Reproduced by permission.

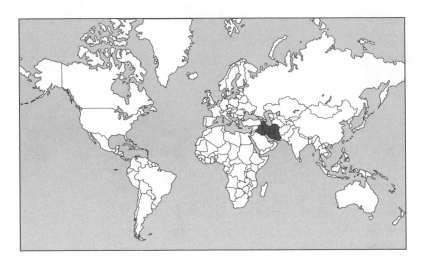

In the approach to the five-year anniversary of the U.S. invasion of Iraq, senior officials from the two most important allies of the new Iraqi government visited Baghdad to mark the occasion. Iranian President Mahmoud Ahmadinejad was greeted by his Iraqi counterparts with all the elaborate pomp and circumstance associated a state visit, the first by an Iranian leader in 30 years and the first of any regional leader since the 2003 invasion. Two weeks later, U.S. Vice President Dick Cheney also made his way to Baghdad. However, despite his infamous pre-war prediction that U.S. forces would be greeted with "sweets and flowers," security conditions forced him to travel under a blanket of secrecy, on a plane carrying a specially reinforced trailer for his sleeping accommodations in a country where 155,000 American troops patrol.

U.S. Mistakes in Understanding Iraq

The contrast between Ahmadinejad's triumphal reception and Cheney's furtive and fortified stopover speaks volumes about the strategic legacy of the Bush administration's decision to use military force to remove the bloody dictatorship of Saddam Hussein. Of the many American illusions and delusions surrounding this war, the administration's calculations with respect to Iran were among the most wildly off base. Instead of generating a liberal, secular democracy whose reverberations would drive out Iran's clerical oligarchs, the disastrous Bush policies fostered a sectarian Iraq that has helped empower Iranian hardliners. Rather than serving as an anchor for a new era of stability and American preeminence in the Persian Gulf, the new Iraq represents a strategic black hole, bleeding Washington of military resources and political influence while extending Iran's primacy among its neighbors.

Like so much else that went wrong in Iraq, the post-war dynamic between Baghdad and Tehran should have been easy to foresee. Iran's leaders cultivated enduring ties with all the significant Iraqi opposition groups over the course of their long adversarial relationship with Saddam Hussein. None of these groups could have been considered wholly-owned clients of the Islamic Republic, but their varying degrees of intimacy with and fealty toward Tehran almost universally surpassed their tactical cooperation with Washington in the run-up to the war and its aftermath. Moreover, as the only organized political forces in the post-war period, the Shia and Kurdish oppositionists were uniquely positioned to take advantage of the power vacuum, facilitated in no small part by retention of their militias.

American officials relied upon the expectation that the two countries' nationalist identities would outweigh any sectarian cohesion, a conclusion supported by the experience of the eight-year Iran-Iraq war. But the U.S. failed to anticipate that in post-war Iraq, sectarian and nationalist interests have been largely conflated for the newly dominant Shia and Kurds, propelling their leaders to utilize the benefits of an alliance with Tehran to entrench their own positions. Moreover, the Bush administration appears to have overestimated the significance of ideology in framing Iran's approach to the new Iraq, hoping that a heavy-handed effort to export the Islamic revolution would alienate Iraqis. Instead, Tehran has behaved far more prudently, opting to support a democratic framework that privileges Iran's allies in Iraq. At the same time, Tehran has sought to increase the cost of a continued American presence in Iraq through support to insurgents, in order to maximize its own position within the country and leverage vis-à-vis Washington.

Iran's strategic and financial investments in Iraq reflect the regime's ... interest in ensuring a friendly government in Baghdad.

The Impact of Iran's Interests

Iran's strategic and financial investments in Iraq reflect the regime's deeply held conviction that Tehran has an existential interest in ensuring a friendly government in Baghdad, one that is no longer capable of threatening Iran directly or on behalf of the international community. For Iran's post-revolutionary leaders and society, the 1980–88 war represents the single most influential formative experience, inculcating a persistent sense of strategic vulnerability and a willingness to do whatever necessary to ensure the survival of both the Iranian nation and the Islamic state. This worldview underlies Tehran's assiduous and wide-ranging extension of influence in post-war Iraq.

As developments repeatedly refuted its initial assumptions about the dynamics between Iraq and Iran, the Bush administration at first sought refuge in denial, absurdly predicting that each new carefully orchestrated leadership transition in Iraq would generate more distance between Tehran and Baghdad. More recently, the administration has moved more forcefully, seeking aggressively to obstruct Iranian support to militias and insurgents. These actions are necessary to ensuring greater security for American forces in Iraq, but ultimately the real means of protecting Iraq's sovereignty from intrusive neighbors does not involve expanding U.S. presence and responsibility within the country. In the long term, Iraqi leaders will only begin to differentiate themselves from Tehran when they are forced to grapple independently with the painful alternatives of governing and assume greater responsibility for their country's security.

There are no magic bullets that will ameliorate the significant setbacks for U.S. interests inherent in the extension of Iran's influence in Iraq.

The Failures of U.S. Policy

In addition, the broader American strategy appears fated to repeat the sort of ill-informed misapprehensions that informed the Bush administration's initial steps in Iraq. In response to growing regional trepidations about Iran's activities in Iraq, Lebanon and Palestine, Washington has endeavored to transform a strategic deficit into an advantage. The concept was catalyzed by the July 2006 war in Lebanon, which Secretary of State Condoleezza Rice characterized at the time as "the birth pangs of a new Middle East." Rice was widely lambasted for her tin ear, but the rhetoric signaled the Administration's decision to embark on building a new platform for America's role in the region. Initiatives such as the Gulf Security Dialogue and GCC-plus-two [Gulf Cooperation Council] discussions (Egypt and Jordan) were intended to capitalize on Sunni Arab concerns about the rising tide of Iranian influence to leverage a more assertive posture vis-à-vis Tehran in exchange for their support for a revived Arab-Israeli peace process.

However, beyond routine exchange of pleasantries and a new stream of arms sales running into the tens of billions of dollars, it is unclear what these initiatives have actually accomplished. Shortly after its rejuvenation at Annapolis, the peace process quickly descended once again into violence, stalemated by the incapacity of both sides to undertake meaningful unilateral concessions. And despite their significant

Iran's Challenges

Despite Iran's undoubted success in embedding itself deeply into Iraqi politics and its continued, almost gleeful defiance of the United States, the European Union, and the IAEA [International Atomic Energy Agency] on the nuclear issue, it would be unwise for Iran's leaders to take their current good luck for granted. The Islamic Republic faces significant social and economic challenges that can only be made more difficult by alienating the key Western industrial countries. The embarrassing and objectionable statements by Iran's new president calling for Israel's destruction have harmed Iran's international image and caused great anxiety at home. Regionally, Iran has poor relations with its Arab neighbors, and it cannot be assumed Iraq's Shiite community will remain friendly and grateful indefinitely. Iran's vital national interests could be helped by ending the standoff with the United States. Likewise, the United States has more to gain than lose if it adopts a more coherent and pragmatic policy toward the Islamic Republic.

Geoffrey Kemp, "Iran and Iraq: The Shia Connection, Soft Power, and the Nuclear Factor: Summary," November 2005. www.usip.org.

misgivings about Iran, the Arab states of the Persian Gulf have made clear—through a series of visits and high-level dialogue—that they will not form the bulwark of an anti-Iranian coalition, even as they privately urge Washington to resolve the Iran problem. For their part, Iran's leaders have demonstrated some awareness of the need to maintain a constructive relationship with Riyadh and the Gulf states, dispatching envoys to Riyadh repeatedly over the past several years to assuage concerns over Ahmadinejad's rhetoric and Iran's escalating tensions with the West.

As with all aspects of the Iraq dilemma, there are no magic bullets that will ameliorate the significant setbacks for U.S. interests inherent in the extension of Iran's influence in Iraq. Five years into this endeavor, neither rhetoric nor alliance-building will enable Washington to reset the clock to 2003. We will have to utilize multiple instruments and approaches to contend with a newly ascendant Iran—containment, active deterrence, and even accommodation and engagement. Tehran has shrewdly exploited the opportunities presented by America's stumbling in Iraq; the challenge for the next Administration will be to acknowledge the realities of regional dynamics and regain the strategic advantage.

Denmark Supported the Invasion of Iraq to Show Solidarity with the United States

Frank Laybourn

In this viewpoint written about six months after the invasion of Iraq, the author, Frank Laybourn, explains the reasons that prompted Denmark to support the U.S.-led coalition. He contends that the September 11, 2001, attacks on the United States demonstrated the ability of terrorists to strike anywhere in the world and that the invasion of Iraq was part of the broader war on terror. The author asserts that Iraq was a threat to the Middle East and could have become a base for future terrorist attacks against the West. Frank Laybourn is an advisor on foreign and security policy for the Danish Liberal Party.

As you read, consider the following questions:

1. According to the viewpoint, has the ability to acquire weapons of mass destruction by terrorists increased or decreased since the September 11, 2001, attacks?
2. What United Nations Security Council Resolution noted that Saddam Hussein was a "threat" to international security?

Frank Laybourn, "Why Denmark Decided to Participate in the War Against Saddam Hussein," September 24, 2003. www.intellectualconservative.com. Reproduced by permission.

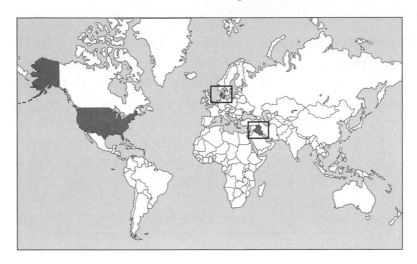

3. According to Laybourn, what are the main reasons listed for the Danes to "show solidarity" with the United States?

International terrorism is a threat to our peace and security, and can strike any country and any population group—including Denmark and the Danes. While terrorism is not new, today's terrorist threat is different from that of the past. The terrorist attacks on the USA on September 11th, 2001, have moved the boundaries. The attacks brutally underlined that the threats posed by international terrorist networks, and the fragile states where they find refuge, are genuine and concern us all. Access to weapons of mass destruction (WMD) and the technologies behind them have become easier.

In September 2002, the Bush administration published its "National Security Strategy," which deals in part with the threat from enemies either possessing or attempting to acquire WMD. "We cannot let our enemies strike first," the administration declares, and states further, "to forestall or prevent (. . .) hostile acts by our adversaries, the Unites States will, if necessary act pre-emptively."

The Danish Government, led by Prime Minister Anders Fogh Rasmussen, shares the US [United States] assessment of the new threats. At NATO's [North Atlantic Treaty Organization's] Prague Summit in November 2002 he declared that, "In today's globalized world, those who do us harm are no longer discouraged by geography or by traditional deterrence. Terrorism, WMD and missiles are the new threats." Moreover, the Danish Government has clearly signaled it believes that the use of military force is a key component of international diplomacy and that the US deserves support in its endeavor to continue its campaign against international terrorism and its roots.

The Danish Government believes the military action was based on sufficient authority and legitimacy under existing resolutions.

The War with Iraq

The war against Iraq should be seen in the context of the principles mentioned above. Firstly, Iraq posed a threat to the regional stability in the Middle East and Central Asia in terms of its continued pursuit of WMD-capability. And if Saddam Hussein acquired nuclear weapons it would have had devastating consequences. We all agreed—including the UN [United Nations] Security Council by its unanimous adoption of Resolution 1441—that Saddam Hussein posed a threat to the international community. Iraq's use of WMD against Iran and the Kurdish minority in Iraq in the 1980s combined with the continued refusal of Saddam Hussein to cooperate with the international community on disarmament simply was not acceptable in a post-9/11 world.

Secondly, one of the lessons learned from leaving Afghanistan unsupervised under the Taliban regime during the 1990s was that rogue states and the rise of so-called power vacuums create safe havens for terrorists and terrorist organizations. In a post 9/11 environment this is not acceptable.

Countries Contributing Troops to the Multinational Force in Iraq as of August 2008

- Albania

- Armenia

- Australia

- Azerbaijan

- Bosnia and Herzegovina

- Bulgaria

- Czech Republic

- Denmark

- El Salvador

- Estonia

- Japan

- Kazakhstan

- South Korea

- Lithuania

- Macedonia

- Mongolia

- Poland

- Romania

- Ukraine

- United Kingdom

Compiled by editor.

Thirdly, the Iraqi regime's continued breach of Security Council resolutions posed a severe threat to the UN's authority in the international system, which the Danish Government could not accept. The Danish Government deeply regrets that it proved impossible to maintain the unity of the Security Council in the face of Saddam Hussein's blatant refusal to render the immediate, active and unconditional cooperation required by Resolution 1441. The months that passed since President Bush made his case in New York on September 12th, 2002, should have been sufficient to deal with Iraq's failure over the preceding twelve years to comply with the demands of the international community. Had the Security Council faced up to its responsibility, the use of force might well have been avoided. Instead, the coalition took action to finish the job that Saddam Hussein never intended to complete. Furthermore, the Danish Government believes the military action was based on sufficient authority and legitimacy under existing resolutions.

Fourthly, we owed the Iraqi population an end to the years of suffering brought upon them by a ruthless dictator. The findings of thousands of bodies in mass graves after the war have only reinforced this notion.

Danish Solidarity with the United States

Finally, but just as importantly, the Danish Government believes that it was right to show solidarity with the United States in its fight against a repressive tyrant. In the last century, the United States has come to our help on numerous occasions. In the First and Second World Wars. By securing our freedom during the Cold War. And by US resolve in the Balkans in the 1990s, when bloody civil wars plagued the region and European leaders were hesitant. We felt that it was our duty to support the United States when the call was—for once—coming from the other side of the Atlantic. As our Prime Minister Anders Fogh Rasmussen stated on March 26

[2003], "Only the Americans have the military strength to disarm Saddam and liberate Iraq. But we have an obligation to help. We cannot just sail under a flag of convenience and let others fight for freedom and peace. There has in fact been too much of that kind in the past in Denmark. If we mean anything seriously about our democratic values, then we should also be ready to make a small contribution to the international coalition."

The purpose of the coalition was to put a stop to reckless and illicit armaments programs and to the ruthless and despotic regime which was responsible for them. Denmark is proud to be part of that coalition. The Danish Government has consistently supported the legitimacy and the necessity of taking action against Saddam Hussein. This was clearly the right and only thing to do and history will prove we were right.

The United States Undermined International Stability When It Invaded Iraq

Hans Blix

In the following viewpoint, Hans Blix strongly criticizes the invasion of Iraq. He asserts that the rationale used for the invasion, that Iraq had weapons of mass destruction, was incorrect. Blix contends that the war undermined international stability and efforts to develop a legal framework for the use of force. He further argues that the United States sent a "dangerous signal" that powerful states could ignore the United Nations (UN). Blix was the chief of UN weapons inspections in Iraq in 2002–2003, and currently is chair of Sweden's Weapons of Mass Destruction Commission.

As you read, consider the following questions:

1. What was the main declared "aim" of the war according to the viewpoint?

2. What does the viewpoint claim might have been an "undeclared" goal of the invasion?

3. In the 2004 U.S. presidential election campaign, what notion did Bush deride?

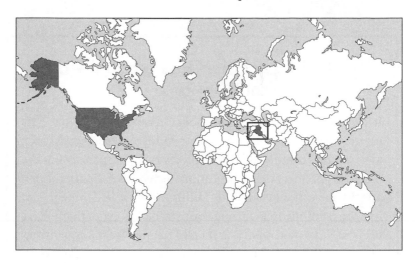

The invasion of Iraq in 2003 was a tragedy—for Iraq, for the US, for the UN, for truth and human dignity. I can only see one gain: the end of Saddam Hussein, a murderous tyrant. Had the war not finished him he would, in all likelihood, have become another Gadafy or Castro; an oppressor of his own people but no longer a threat to the world. Iraq was on its knees after a decade of sanctions.

The elimination of weapons of mass destruction was the declared main aim of the war. It is improbable that the governments of the alliance could have sold the war to their parliaments on any other grounds. That they believed in the weapons' existence in the autumn of 2002 is understandable. Why had the Iraqis stopped UN inspectors during the 90s if they had nothing to hide? Responsibility for the war must rest, though, on what those launching it knew by March 2003.

By then, UNMOVIC [United Nations Monitoring, Verification and Inspection Commission] inspectors had carried out some 700 inspections at 500 sites without finding prohibited weapons. The contract that George Bush held up before Congress to show that Iraq was purchasing uranium oxide

---

The Iraq Invasion Has Led to the Use of Chemical Weapons

It has been reported in the media recently that insurgents in Iraq have been utilizing toxic industrial chemicals such as chlorine (combined with explosives for dispersal) for the purpose of harming the unprotected population. Such attacks have resulted in the killing of tens and injuring of hundreds of people throughout Iraq. To date there have been at least ten reported attacks using various quantities of chlorine, while several other attempted attacks using chlorine and other toxic products have reportedly been foiled by the security forces.

United Nations, "Twenty-Ninth Quarterly Report on the Activities of the United Nations Monitoring, Verification and Inspection Commission in Accordance with Paragraph 12 of Security Council Resolution 1284 (1999)," May 29, 2007. www.un.org.

---

was proved to be a forgery. The allied powers were on thin ice, but they preferred to replace question marks with exclamation marks.

They could not succeed in eliminating WMDs because they did not exist. Nor could they succeed in the declared aim to eliminate al-Qaida operators, because they were not in Iraq.

They could not succeed in eliminating WMDs because they did not exist. Nor could they succeed in the declared aim to eliminate al-Qaida operators, because they were not in Iraq. They came later, attracted by the occupants. A third declared aim was to bring democracy to Iraq, hopefully becoming an example for the region. Let us hope for the future; but five years of occupation has clearly brought more anarchy than democracy.

Increased safety for Israel might have been an undeclared US aim. If so, it is hard to see that anything was gained by a war which has strengthened Iran.

There are other troubling legacies of the Iraq war. It is a setback in the world's efforts to develop legal restraints on the use of armed force between states. In 1945, the US helped to write into the UN charter a prohibition of the use of armed force against states. Exceptions were made only for self-defence against armed attacks and for armed force authorised by the security council. In 2003, Iraq was not a real or imminent threat to anybody. Instead, the invasion reflects a claim made in the 2002 US national security strategy that the charter was too restrictive, and that the US was ready to use armed force to meet threats that were uncertain as to time and place—a doctrine of preventive war.

In the 2004 presidential election campaign, Bush ridiculed any idea that the US would need to ask for a "permission slip" before taking military action against a "growing threat". True, the 2003 Iraq invasion is not the only case in which armed force has been used in disregard of the charter. However, from the most powerful member of the UN it is a dangerous signal. If preventive war is accepted for one, it is accepted for all.

One fear is that the UN rules ignored in the attack on Iraq will prove similarly insignificant in the case of Iran. But it may be that the spectacular failure of ensuring disarmament by force, and of introducing democracy by occupation, will work in favour of a greater use of diplomacy and "soft power". Justified concerns about North Korea and Iran have led the US, as well as China, Russia and European states, to examine what economic and other non-military inducements they may use to ensure that these two states do not procure nuclear weapons. Washington and Moscow must begin nuclear disarmament. So long as these nuclear states maintain that these weapons are indispensable to their security, it is not surprising that others may think they are useful. What, really, is the alternative: invasion and occupation, as in Iraq?

The United States' Invasion of Iraq Was a Positive Development for International Relations

Robert Kagan and William Kristol

In the viewpoint below, authors Robert Kagan and William Kristol argue in favor of the Iraq invasion. They discount the assertion that United Nations weapons inspectors should have been granted more time to examine Iraq's weapons of mass destruction program before the onset of war. The authors assert that the main reasons for war included Saddam's defiance of international conventions and his ties to terrorists. Robert Kagan is the author of Dangerous Nation: America's Place in the World from Its Earliest Days to the Dawn of the Twentieth Century, *and William Kristol is the editor of* The Weekly Standard.

As you read, consider the following questions:

1. According to the viewpoint, what were the main reasons, besides the threat of weapons of mass destruction, to go to war?

2. What does the viewpoint claim was the main purpose for United Nations Security Council Resolution 1441?

3. In David Kay's report, what were the major examples of Iraq's ongoing weapons of mass destruction program?

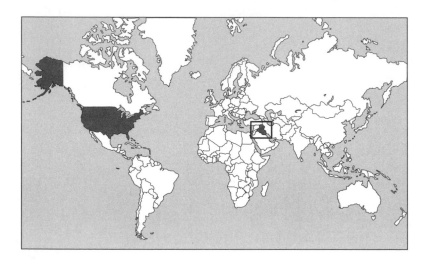

W as it right to go to war?

Critics of the war, and of the [George W.] Bush administration, have seized on the failure to find stockpiles of weapons of mass destruction [WMD] in Iraq. But while his weapons were a key part of the case for removing Saddam, that case was always broader. Saddam's pursuit of weapons of mass destruction was inextricably intertwined with the nature of his tyrannical rule, his serial aggression, his defiance of international obligations, and his undeniable ties to a variety of terrorists, from Abu Nidal to al Qaeda. . . . Together, this pattern of behavior made the removal of Saddam desirable and necessary, in the judgment of both the Clinton and Bush administrations. That judgment was and remains correct. . . .

The Impact of 9/11

September 11 [2001 terrorist attacks on the United States] shocked the nation, and it shocked the president. Its effect was to make many both inside and outside the administration take a closer look at international threats, because it was clear that all of us had been too sanguine about such threats prior to September 11. Nor was it in the least surprising that the issue of Iraq arose immediately. True, neither candidate in the 2000 election had talked much about Iraq. But that was not because anyone believed it had ceased to be an urgent and growing problem. The Clinton administration didn't want to talk about it because it felt it had run out of options. The Bush campaign didn't talk about it because Bush was running a campaign, ironic in retrospect, which promised a less active, more restrained American role in the world. But that did not mean the Iraq issue had gone away, and after September 11, it returned to the fore. After all, we had a decade-long history of confrontation with Iraq, we were flying military missions in Iraqi air space, President Clinton had declared Saddam the greatest threat to our security in the 21st century, Clinton officials like Sandy Berger and Madeleine Albright had concluded that Saddam must eventually be removed, and U.N. [United Nations] weapons inspectors had written one alarming report after another about Saddam's current and potential weapons capabilities.

So the Bush administration concluded that it had to remove the Saddam Hussein regime once and for all, just as Clinton and Berger had suggested might someday be necessary. For all the reasons that Berger had outlined, Saddam's regime itself was the problem, above and beyond his weapons capabilities. It was an obstacle to progress in the Middle East and the Arab world. It was a threat to the Iraqi people and to Iraq's neighbors. But a big part of the threat involved Saddam's absolute determination to arm himself with both conventional and unconventional weapons.

A majority of Democratic Senators—including, of course, John Kerry and John Edwards—voted for the resolution authorizing the president to use force against Iraq.

September 11 had added new dimensions to the danger. For as Bush and many others argued, what if Saddam allowed his weapons capabilities to be shared with terrorists? What if, someday in the future, terrorists like those who crashed airplanes into the World Trade Center [in New York City] and the Pentagon [in Washington, D.C.] had nuclear, chemical, or biological weapons? Would they hesitate to use them? The possible nexus between terrorism and Iraq's weapons program made Iraq an even more urgent issue. Was this concern farfetched? If so, it was exactly the same far-fetched concern that had preoccupied President Clinton in 1998, when he warned, in his speech on Iraq, about a "rogue state with weapons of mass destruction, ready to use them or provide them to terrorists," and when he had spoken of an "unholy axis" of international terrorists and outlaw states as one of the greatest threats Americans faced.

Nor was it surprising that as President Bush began to move toward war with Iraq in the fall and winter of 2002, he mustered substantial support among Democrats as well as Republicans. A majority of Democratic senators—including, of course, John Kerry and John Edwards—voted for the resolution authorizing the president to use force against Iraq. And why not? The Bush administration's approach to Iraq was fundamentally in keeping with that of the Clinton administration, except that after September 11, inaction seemed even less acceptable. The majority of the Democratic party foreign policy establishment supported the war, and not because they were misled by the Bush administration's rhetorical hype leading up to the war. (Its hype was appreciably less than that of Clinton secretary of defense William Cohen, who appeared on national television in late 1997 holding a bag of sugar and noting that the same amount of anthrax "would destroy at least half the population" of Washington, D.C. At a Pentagon press briefing on Iraq's WMD, Cohen also noted that if Saddam had "as much VX [a nerve agent] in storage as the U.N. suspects," he would "be able to kill every human being on the face of the planet.") Nor did they support the war because they were fundamentally misled by American intelligence about the nature and extent of Saddam's weapons programs. Most of what they and everyone else knew about those programs we had learned from the U.N. inspectors, not from U.S. intelligence.

The whole inspections regime was premised on Saddam's cooperation. But Saddam never cooperated, not in the 1990s and not in 2003.

Weapons of Mass Destruction

Some of that intelligence has now turned out to be wrong. Some of it has turned out to be right. And it is simply too soon to tell about the rest. The press has focused attention almost entirely on [former U.N. weapons inspector] David Kay's assertion that there were no stockpiles of chemical and biological weapons when the United States and its allies invaded Iraq last March [2003]. We'll address that assertion in a moment. But what about the rest of Kay's testimony?

The key question for more than a decade, for both the Clinton and the Bush administrations, was not only what weapons Saddam had but what weapons he was trying to obtain, and how long it might be before containment failed and he was able to obtain them. The goal of American policy, and indeed of the U.N. Security Council over the course of the dozen years after the end of the Gulf War in 1991, was not primarily to find Saddam's existing stockpiles. That was subsidiary to the larger goal, which was to achieve Iraq's disarmament, including the elimination not only of existing prohibited weapons but of all such weapons programs, to ensure that Iraq would not possess weapons of mass destruction now or in the future. As Richard Butler and other weapons inspectors have argued, this task proved all but impossible once it became clear that Saddam was determined to acquire such weapons at some point. As Butler repeated time and again in

"Take this, Saddam! And this! Well, I hope it hurts, Man! No mercy!" cartoon by Karsten Schley. Www.Cartoonstock.com.

his reports to the Security Council, the whole inspections regime was premised on Saddam's cooperation. But Saddam never cooperated, not in the 1990s and not in 2003.

U.N. Security Council Resolution 1441

It is important to recall that the primary purpose of Security Council Resolution 1441, passed on November 8, 2002, was not to discover whether Saddam had weapons and programs. There was little doubt that Saddam had them. The real question was whether he was ready to make a clean breast of everything and give up not only his forbidden weapons but also his efforts to acquire them once and for all. The purpose was to give Saddam "one final chance" to change his stripes, to offer full cooperation by revealing and dismantling all his programs and to forswear all such efforts in the future.

After all, what would be accomplished if Saddam turned over stockpiles and dismantled programs, only to restart them the minute the international community turned its back? Saddam might be slowed, but he would not be stopped. This was the logic that had led the Clinton administration to conclude that someday, somehow, the only answer to the problem would be Saddam's removal from power. Not surprisingly, the Bush administration was even more convinced that Saddam's removal was the only answer. That the administration went along with the inspections process embodied in Resolution 1441 was a concession to international and domestic pressure. No senior official, including Secretary [of State Colin] Powell, believed there was any but the smallest chance Saddam would comply with the terms of Resolution 1441.

We know ... definitively that Saddam did not comply with Resolution 1441.

Resolution 1441 demanded that, within 30 days, Iraq provide "a currently accurate, full, and complete declaration of all aspects of its programs to develop chemical, biological, and nuclear weapons, ballistic missiles, and other delivery systems such as unmanned aerial vehicles and dispersal systems designed for use on aircraft, including any holdings and precise locations of such weapons, components, sub-components, stocks of agents, and related material and equipment, the locations and work of its research, development and production facilities, as well as all other chemical, biological, and nuclear programs, including any which it claims are for purposes not related to weapon production or material." Administration officials doubted Saddam would do this. They hoped only that, once Saddam's noncompliance became clear, they would win unanimous support for war at the U.N. Security Council.

Saddam's Failure to Comply with the U.N.

And it was pretty clear at the time that Saddam was not complying. In his May 30, 2003, report to the Security Council, Hans Blix reported that the declared stocks of anthrax and VX remained unaccounted for. And he elaborated: "Little progress was made in the solution of outstanding issues. . . . The long list of proscribed items unaccounted for and as such resulting in unresolved disarmament issues was not shortened either by the inspections or by Iraqi declarations and documentation."

Now, of course, we know more definitively that Saddam did not comply with Resolution 1441. That is a part of Kay's testimony that has been widely ignored. What Kay discovered in the course of his eight-month-long investigation was that Iraq had failed to answer outstanding questions about its arsenal and programs. Indeed, it had continued to engage in an elaborate campaign of deception and concealment of weapons activities throughout the time when Hans Blix and the UN-MOVIC [United Nations Monitoring, Verification, and Inspection Commission] inspectors were in the country, and right up until the day of the invasion, and beyond.

As Kay told the Senate Armed Services Committee last month [January 2004], the Iraq Survey Group "discovered hundreds of cases, based on both documents, physical evidence and the testimony of Iraqis, of activities that were prohibited under the initial U.N. Resolution 687 and that should have been reported under 1441, with Iraqi testimony that not only did they not tell the U.N. about this, they were instructed not to do it and they hid material." Kay reported, "We have had a number of Iraqis who have come forward and said, 'We did not tell the U.N. about what we were hiding, nor would we have told the U.N.,'" because the risks were too great. And what were the Iraqis hiding? As Kay reports, "They maintained programs and activities, and they certainly had the intentions at a point to resume their programs. So there was a lot they wanted to hide because it showed what they were doing was illegal." As Kay reported last October [2003], his survey team uncovered "dozens of WMD-related program activities and significant amounts of equipment that Iraq concealed from the U.N. during the inspections that began in late 2002." Specifically, Kay reported:

- A clandestine network of laboratories and safehouses within the Iraqi Intelligence Service that contained equipment suitable for research in the production of chemical and biological weapons. This kind of equipment was explicitly mentioned in Hans Blix's requests for information, but was instead concealed from Blix throughout his investigations.

- A prison laboratory complex, which may have been used in human testing of biological weapons agents. Iraqi officials working to prepare for U.N. inspections in 2002 and 2003 were explicitly ordered not to acknowledge the existence of the prison complex.

- So-called "reference strains" of biological organisms, which can be used to produce biological weapons. The strains were found in a scientist's home.

- New research on agents applicable to biological weapons, including Congo Crimean Hemorrhagic Fever, and continuing research on [toxins] ricin and aflatoxin—all of which was, again, concealed from Hans Blix despite his specific request for any such information.

- Plans and advanced design work on new missiles with ranges up to at least 1,000 kilometers—well beyond the 150-kilometer limit imposed on Iraq by the U.N. Security Council. These missiles would have allowed Saddam to threaten targets from Ankara to Cairo.

Last month [January 2004] Kay also reported that Iraq "was in the early stages of renovating the [nuclear] program, building new buildings."

As Kay has testified repeatedly, Iraq was "in clear material violation of 1441." So if the world had known in February 2003 what Kay says we know now—that there were no large stockpiles of weapons, but that Iraq continued to pursue weapons of mass destruction programs and to deceive and conceal these efforts from the U.N. inspectors led by Blix during the time allocated by Resolution 1441—wouldn't there have been at least as much, and probably more, support for the war? For Saddam would have been in flagrant violation of yet another set of commitments to disarm. He would have demonstrated once again that he was unwilling to abandon these programs, that he was unwilling to avail himself of this "last chance" and disarm once and for all. Had the world discovered unambiguously in February 2003 that Saddam was cheating on its commitments in Resolution 1441, surely even the French would have found it difficult to block a U.N. resolution authorizing war. As Dominique de Villepin acknowledged in the contentious months before the war, "We all realize that success in the inspections presupposes that we get full and complete cooperation from Iraq." What if it were as clear then as it is now that Saddam was engaged in another round of deceit and concealment? . . .

It is very unlikely that, given another three months or six months, the Blix team would have come to any definitive conclusion one way or another.

Why Not Give Inspections More Time?

There was an argument against going to war last year [2003]. But let's remember what that argument was. It had nothing to do with whether or not Saddam had weapons of mass destruction and WMD programs. Everyone from Howard Dean to the *New York Times* editorial board to Dominique de Villepin and Jacques Chirac assumed that he had both. Most of the arguments against the war concerned timing. The most frequent complaint was that Bush was rushing to war. Why not give Blix and his inspectors another three months or six months?

We now know, however, that giving Blix a few more months would not have made a difference. Last month Kay was asked what would have happened if Blix and his team had been allowed to continue their mission. Kay responded, "All I can say is that among an extensive body of Iraqi scientists who are talking to us, they have said: The U.N. interviewed us; we did not tell them the truth, we did not show them this equipment, we did not talk about these programs; we couldn't do it as long as Saddam was in power. I suspect regardless of how long they had stayed, that attitude would have been the same." Given the "terror regime of Saddam," Kay concluded, he and his team learned things after the war "that no U.N. inspector would have ever learned" while Saddam was still in power.

So it is very unlikely that, given another three months or six months, the Blix team would have come to any definitive conclusion one way or another. Nor, therefore, would there have been a much greater probability of winning a unanimous vote at the Security Council for war once those additional six months had passed. Whether the United States could have kept 200,000 troops on a permanent war footing in the Persian Gulf for another six months is even more doubtful.

> *As Senate Democratic leader Tom Daschle said . . . 'The threat posed by Saddam Hussein may not be imminent, but it is real, it is growing and it cannot be ignored.'*

The Claim That Iraq's Threat Was Imminent

Did the administration claim the Iraqi threat was imminent, in the sense that Iraq possessed weapons that were about to be used against the United States? That is the big charge leveled by the Bush administration's critics these days. It is rather surprising, given the certainty with which this charge is thrown around, how little the critics have in the way of quotations from administration officials to back it up. Saying that action is urgent is not the same thing as saying the threat is imminent. In fact, the president said the threat was not imminent, and that we had to act (urgently) before the threat became imminent. This was well understood. As Senate Democratic leader Tom Daschle said on October 10, 2002, explaining his support for the legislation authorizing the president to go to war, "The threat posed by Saddam Hussein may not be imminent, but it is real, it is growing and it cannot be ignored."

One reason critics have been insisting that the administration claimed the threat from Iraq was imminent, we believe, is that it is fairly easy to prove that the danger to the United States was not imminent. But the central thesis of the antiwar argument as it was advanced before the war asserted that the threat from Iraq would not have been imminent even if Saddam had possessed every conceivable weapon in his arsenal. Remember, the vast majority of arguments against the war assumed that he did have these weapons. But those weapons, it was argued, did not pose an imminent threat to the nation because Saddam, like the Soviet Union, could be deterred. Indeed, the fact that he had the weapons, some argued, was all the more reason why the United States should not go to war. After all, it was argued, the likeliest scenario for Saddam's actually using the weapons he had was in the event of an American invasion. The current debate over "imminence" is an ex post facto attempt to relitigate the old argument over the war. The non-discovery of weapons stockpiles has not changed the contours of that debate. . . .

War Was Unavoidable

We believe that war would have come eventually because of the trajectory that Saddam was on—assuming the United

States intended to continue to play its role as guarantor of peace and security in the Middle East. The question was whether it was safer to act sooner or later. The president argued, convincingly, that it was safer—it was necessary—to act sooner. Sanctions could not have been maintained; containment, already dubious, was far less persuasive after September 11; and so the war to remove Saddam was, in the broad strategic sense, in the sense relevant to serious international politics, necessary. This is of course a legitimate subject of debate—but it would be almost as much so even if large stockpiles of weapons had already been recovered. . . .

Whatever the results of [Kay's] search, it will continue to be the case that the war was worth fighting, and that it was necessary. For the people of Iraq, the war put an end to three decades of terror and suffering. The mass graves uncovered since the end of the war are alone sufficient justification for it. Assuming the United States remains committed to helping establish a democratic government in Iraq, that will be a blessing both to the Iraqi people and to their neighbors. As for those neighbors, the threat of Saddam's aggression, which hung over the region for more than two decades, has finally been eliminated. The prospects for war in the region have been substantially diminished by our action.

It is also becoming clear that the battle of Iraq has been an important victory in the broader war in which we are engaged, a war against terror, against weapons proliferation, and for a new Middle East. Already, other terror-implicated regimes in the region that were developing weapons of mass destruction are feeling pressure, and some are beginning to move in the right direction. Libya has given up its weapons of mass destruction program. Iran has at least gestured toward opening its nuclear program to inspection. The clandestine international network organized by Pakistan's A.Q. Khan that has been so central to nuclear proliferation to rogue states has been exposed. From Iran to Saudi Arabia, liberal forces seem to have been encouraged. We are paying a real price in blood and treasure in Iraq. But we believe that it is already clear—as clear as such things get in the real world—that the price of the liberation of Iraq has been worth it.

Periodical Bibliography

The following articles have been selected to supplement the diverse views presented in this chapter.

Jason W. Davidson "In and Out of Iraq: A Vote-Seeking Explanation of Berlusconi's Iraq Policy," *Modern Italy*, February 2008.

Alexander R. Dawoody "Examining the Preemptive War in Iraq," *Public Integrity*, Winter 2006/2007.

Robert Dreyfuss "End of Iraq's Awakening?" *The Nation*, September 30, 2008.

Jeffrey Goldberg "After Iraq," *The Atlantic*, January/February 2008.

John Grey "A Modest Defense of the President and His Policies of Creative Destruction," *New Statesman*, January 17, 2005.

Joshua Muravchik "Iraq and the Conservatives," *Commentary*, October 2005.

Cornelius F. Murphy Jr. "The Role of International Moral Authority in Iraq," *America*, July 2, 2007.

New Statesman "Iraq: The Issue We Have Chosen to Forget," June 27, 2005.

Kevin Peraino "The Man in the Middle," *Newsweek*, December 31, 2007.

Robert J. Pranger "American Foreign Policy After Iraq," *Mediterranean Quarterly*, Summer 2008.

Martin Van Creveld "The Fall: Consequences of US Withdrawal from Iraq," *NPQ: New Perspectives Quarterly*, Winter 2007.

Mortimer Zuckerman "Seeing the Job Through," *U.S. News and World Report*, December 12, 2005.

CHAPTER 2

The Iraq War and the Arab-Israeli Conflict

The United States and France Have Different Approaches to Iraq and the Arab-Israeli Conflict

Justin Vaisse

In the following viewpoint, Justin Vaisse argues that even though relations between the United States and France have improved since 2007, there remain deep differences between the two countries on Iraq and the Arab-Israeli conflict. For instance, Vaisse argues that U.S. policy is often too pro-Israel and that affects other issues in the region, including Iraq and Lebanon. Vaisse is a senior fellow on Foreign Policy at the Brookings Institution and the author of Integrating Islam: Political and Religious Challenges in contemporary France.

As you read, consider the following questions:

1. According to the viewpoint, what is the major difference between France and the United States on the "link" between al Qaeda and Palestinian terrorism?

2. What issue prompted the United States and France to restart "active cooperation" in 2004?

3. What does the viewpoint assert is the main difference between U.S. and French policy on the creation of a Palestinian state?

Justin Vaisse, "The Arab-Israeli Conflict as a Franco-American Challenge," Brookings Institution, November 18, 2007. www.brookings.edu. Reproduced by permission of the author.

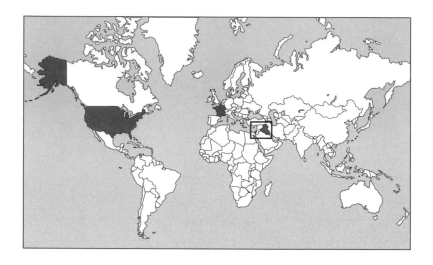

It would be an understatement to say that France and the United States have not always seen eye-to-eye with each other on the Arab-Israeli conflict. Indeed, this issue has caused some of the most vitriolic diplomatic disputes between Paris and Washington of the last decades, especially in the 1970s.

A Thaw in France-US Relations

More recently, however, the scope of disagreement has tended to narrow, and has given way to increased understanding and cooperation. This was certainly the case during the Oslo Peace Process years (1993–2000), this was largely the case during the first few months of the Road Map initiative undertaken by the Quartet (2003) [the United States, Russia, the European Union, and the United Nations], and this has also been the case in the recent months, with the efforts led by Secretary of State Condoleezza Rice to revive the dialogue between the two parties. As a symbol of this convergence, French Foreign Minister Bernard Kouchner recently offered to host a donors' conference in Paris to complement the peace conference scheduled to take place in Annapolis later this month [November 2007].

Does this mean that France and the US are now in complete agreement on this issue? Does the replacement of President Jacques Chirac by Nicolas Sarkozy—who did not hesitate to trumpet his friendship not only for the US, but for Israel as well, during the presidential campaign—usher in a new era of agreement on the Arab-Israeli conflict? If there are reasons to be optimistic, expectations should not get out of hand, as divergences in analysis and interests remain, and the situation on the ground is, in any case, both messy and worrying. Before getting to the specifics of agreements and disagreements between France and the United States, it is useful to review the events of the past few years from a Franco-American perspective.

Regime change in Iraq would 'serve as a dramatic and inspiring example of freedom for other nations in the region,' including the Palestinians, in the words of President Bush.

The Bush Approach

The "hands-off" approach adopted by the Bush administration toward the Israeli-Palestinian conflict—a strong contrast with the policy of its predecessor—was a cause of great concern in Paris. In spite of the short-lived hope generated by the Road Map, French-US perceptions of the Middle East have been marked by divergence, on three issues at least.

First, the primacy of the Israeli-Palestinian peace process for the whole region, a strongly held view in Paris, was disputed by the Bush administration. Many inside this administration considered other regional problems as more critical—especially, it soon turned out, the lack of freedom and democracy, most notably in Iraq. "The road to Jerusalem goes through Baghdad", rather than the reverse French view, was the slogan encapsulating this argument in 2002–2003, with the hope that regime change in Iraq would "serve as a dramatic and inspiring example of freedom for other nations in the region," including the Palestinians, in the words of President Bush in February 2003.

The second issue was the conceptual link established by the Bush administration between al Qaeda and Palestinian terrorist groups, in the context of a "global war on terror" in which the US, Israel, and the rest of the civilized world faced a single, monolithic enemy. Seen from Paris, if terrorism from any source is always to be strongly condemned, this view was analytically wrong and politically damaging. In contrast to al Qaeda, with which it is not possible to negotiate anything, Palestinians have legitimate political objectives, and the strategy should be to dissociate the terrorists or armed branch from the moderates or political branch—with which a settlement will ultimately be found. By lumping al Qaeda and Palestinians together, the "global war on terror" de-legitimizes Palestinian claims and ultimately plays into the hands of the radicals.

The third issue is closely related to the second, and has to do with the strength of the Palestinian leadership. Paris had supported Yasser Arafat in the past, certainly not because he was a flawless leader, but out of conviction that lasting peace could only be achieved through direct talks between the two enemies recognizing each other's existence and legitimacy. Ariel Sharon's siege of Arafat's Ramallah headquarters in 2001–2002, George W. Bush's prerequisite that Yasser Arafat goes away before anything happens, the lack of support for Mahmoud Abbas when he succeeded Arafat, the unilateral nature of Sharon's withdrawal from Gaza, the insistence that Palestinians hold free and fair elections in January 2006 but the refusal to accept the consequences of their outcome: all these decisions gave the impression that Israel, the United States and, sometimes, the international community, were ready to take Palestinians seriously only if they underwent radical change to their liking. The problem is that in order to have a peace process, you need a moderate, solid and legitimate Palestinian leadership to negotiate with—but in order to get this kind of leadership, you need a peace process.

Paris ... while considering Hamas to be a terrorist organization, holds that it can change in the future—as the PLO did in 1989.

Contemporary Differences (2001–2006)

The building of the West Bank barrier, while justifiable on security grounds, was criticized by Paris and the international community, and to a much lesser extent by the US, in as much as it did not go along the Green Line (the 1949 Armistice Line) but cut into the West Bank, and reduced Palestinians' ability to move around, work or cultivate their fields, thereby radicalizing many.

While George W. Bush accepted Sharon's unilateral disengagement plan from Gaza in 2004–2005, Paris and the EU [European Union] as a whole were ambivalent at first, not only as a matter of principle (peace cannot be achieved unilaterally, and priority should be given to the Road Map), but also out of concern that this could impede the peace process for many years and lead to an acceleration of construction of settlements in the West Bank, as comments by Dov Weisglass, a senior aide to Sharon—and subsequent developments since 2005—have seemed to confirm. However, France and the EU, inside the Quartet, gradually warmed up to the idea and supported it, provided this would be a first step towards a more permanent settlement of the Israeli-Palestinian conflict.

Reaction to Hamas [a Palestinian Sunni paramilitary organization] victory in January 2006 was as firm in Paris as it was in Washington. The Quartet asked the new government to recognize Israel as one of the preconditions for continuing development aid. Paris, however, while considering Hamas to be

---

France's Symbolic Visit to Iraq

France's foreign minister paid an unannounced and highly symbolic visit to Baghdad on Sunday [August 2007]—the first by a senior French official since the war started and a gesture to the American effort in Iraq after years of icy relations over the U.S.-led invasion. Bernard Kouchner said Paris wanted to "turn the page" and look to the future. . . .

"Now we are turning the page. There is a new perspective. We want to talk about the future. Democracy, integrity, sovereignty, reconciliation and stopping the killings. That's my deep aim," Kouchner said in English after meeting with Iraqi Foreign Minister Hosyhar Zebari.

Kim Gamel, "France Offers U.S. Symbol with Iraq Trip," Boston Globe, August 19, 2007. www.boston.com.

---

a terrorist organization, holds that it can change in the future—as the PLO did in 1989—and possibly become, once it has recognized Israel and renounced terrorism, a party to negotiate with, while—despite statements to the contrary—Washington acts as if it did not consider this possible.

There are more than 800,000 Francophones in Israel, France is the 6th largest trading partner of Tel Aviv, and people-to-people exchanges are extremely dense.

When the war in Lebanon broke out in July 2006, Washington expressed its tacit support, hoping that Hezbollah would be significantly weakened. Paris was more doubtful on this point, and feared that a disproportionate reaction would have terrible effects on the population of Lebanon as a whole. To take the Israeli concern into account, Paris and other European capitals took the lead in reinforcing the UNIFIL [United Nations Interim Force in Lebanon] to better act as a buffer force in Southern Lebanon, under UNSC [United Nations Security Council] 1701.

Franco-American Divergences and Convergences Today

Is Nicolas Sarkozy's view of the region very different from that of Jacques Chirac? The two men don't belong to the same generation, and they certainly don't have the same personal ties and experience in the region. In contrast with Chirac's old friendships with many Arab leaders, Nicolas Sarkozy has made clear that he is a friend of Israel—and he is celebrated as such in Tel Aviv and in Washington.

However, a closer look reveals that during the campaign, Nicolas Sarkozy used the same rhetorical device he used vis-à-vis the US, namely "I am a friend of the US/of Israel ... but real friends tell real friends what they think". And what he thinks does not necessarily coincide with what Americans and/or Israelis would like to hear. For example, he described Israel's war against Hezbollah in the summer of 2006 as "clumsy and disproportionate", the exact code words used by the Quai d'Orsay. It should be noted, moreover, that starting with the recommendations of a blue-ribbon group of experts in 2002, aggressive steps have been taken under Jacques Chirac to improve Franco-Israeli relations (after all, there are more than 800,000 Francophones in Israel, France is the 6th largest trading partner of Tel Aviv, and people-to-people exchanges are extremely dense), resulting in a marked improvement of diplomatic ties, symbolized by frequent high-level and successful visits of Prime Ministers Sharon then Ehud Olmert in the past two years. Since he took office in May 2007, Nicolas Sarkozy has not noticeably changed France's stance in the region, and has—so far—followed in the footsteps of Jacques Chirac.

So if Sarkozy has not substantially altered French foreign policy, what are the current points of agreement and disagreement between the US and France on the Arab-Israeli conflict?

- At base, there is a strong French-US agreement on the question of security for Israel and condemnation of Palestinian terrorism.

- The convergence on Iran has been remarkable. Nicolas Sarkozy has been vocal in stating that an Iranian nuclear bomb was not acceptable, but Jacques Chirac, before him, had taken a hard line on Iran. This brings the question of the Shia—Sunni rift which has come to dominate the region, whether in Iraq, in Lebanon, or indirectly in the Palestinian territories. On the necessity to contain radical Iranian influence in all of these places, and work with the traditional regional allies, Paris and Washington are in agreement.

- The fate of Lebanon and the adoption of a hard line on Syria was, in 2004, one of the first issues on which France and the US resumed active cooperation, with UNSC resolution 1559 and, in May 2006, resolution 1680. . . .

The Bush administration now advocates the creation of a Palestinian state, while France always insists that it must be a viable *Palestinian state, not a patchwork of remote pieces of land.*

Enduring French-US Differences

As mentioned above, Paris is convinced that peace can only come through a process of negotiations between the two enemies, which means that moderate Palestinian leaders such as Mahmoud Abbas should not be sidestepped, and that they should be helped—and not only a few months before the elections, as was seen in the past. Too often in the recent years, Palestinian leaders have been criticized or undercut, especially by the US Congress, and this has been detrimental to the peace process. This rationale is behind France's proposal to host a donors' conference in Paris later this year. The conference will be presided over by Tony Blair, the special envoy of the Quartet, who shares this goal of reinforcing Mahmoud Abbas and Prime Minister Salam Fayyad. It is crucial that Mahmoud Abbas be reinforced not only in the donors' conference, but in Annapolis as well—a failure to do so would only comfort Hamas, which controls Gaza since June 2007 and is threatening Abbas's rule in the West Bank.

Another aim of the Paris conference is to provide more help to the Palestinian population, who has suffered greatly in recent years, especially in Gaza, where the situation is now close to a humanitarian catastrophe. Paris voices its concern more often than Washington on this issue, and has been providing substantial financial and humanitarian help along with the EU throughout the recent years, because increasing poverty and despair can only lead to further radicalization and embrace of Hamas. Thus for example the Quai d'Orsay reacted negatively on October 29, 2007, when Israeli sanctions against civilians in the Gaza strip (on electricity and fuel supplies) were tightened.

The Bush administration now advocates the creation of a Palestinian state, while France always insists that it must be a *viable* Palestinian state, not a patchwork of remote pieces of land. France has been much more vocal than Washington about the uninterrupted growth of illegal settlements in occupied territory, especially in East Jerusalem, which will make a final peace agreement more difficult and threaten the viability of the future state. Of particular concern has been the Maale Adounim settlement and the "E1 zone" project, which separates the Northern from the Southern West Bank. Indeed, on November 18, 2007, while traveling to the region, Bernard

Kouchner [France's foreign minister] declared that "colonization is not only contrary to law, it is also the main obstacle to peace from a political point of view."

The last disagreement has to do with Lebanon. While there is real convergence on this issue, as previously mentioned, France is more concerned with issues of Lebanese domestic politics, while Washington seems more focused on countering Syria there. A good example of this disagreement can be found in the attitude towards Hezbollah, which Washington considers only as a terrorist organization, and which Paris sees also as a political force in Lebanese politics that must be reckoned with. This is why Bernard Kouchner and Nicolas Sarkozy included Hezbollah in the talks at La Celle-Saint-Cloud in July 2007 (aiming at fostering a solution to the political deadlock), a move that triggered an angry letter from the US Congress to Nicolas Sarkozy, authored by Rep. Robert Wexler and signed by 91 of his colleagues. In the recent months, a special advisor to Bernard Kouchner, Jean-Claude Cousseran, and two special representatives of President Sarkozy, Claude Guéant and Jean-David Lévitte, were sent to Damascus to discuss the coming presidential elections.

A word about perceptions to complete the picture. Enduring stereotypes persist in both countries about the other country's stance on the conflict. For example, the French tend to believe that the US and Israel are always in agreement, while the situation is much more conflictual—it is actually often frustrating, as viewed from Washington. The pro-Israeli lobby is sometimes credited with more influence than it has. Americans, on their part, tend to think that France is reflexively pro-Palestinian, they sometimes distrust French sentiments vis-à-vis the security of Israel, and they ignore the depth and quality of the relationship between Paris and Tel Aviv.

To conclude, there is no doubt that renewed engagement on the part of the Bush administration has been welcomed by

Paris and the EU in general, which can more easily associate itself with this policy. As Nicolas Sarkozy said to the US Congress on November 7, 2007: "To the Israeli and Palestinian leaders I say this: Don't hesitate! Risk peace! And do it now! The status quo hides even greater dangers: that of delivering Palestinian society as a whole to the extremists that contest Israel's existence."

The Arab-Israeli Conflict Must Be Resolved to Achieve U.S. Goals in the Middle East

Patrick Seale

In this viewpoint, Patrick Seale contends that the United States faces massive defeat in Iraq unless it adopts a new strategy. He asserts that the actions of the United States and Israel have actually increased tensions in the Middle East. Seale argues that the best policy for the United States is to attempt to resolve the Arab-Israeli conflict, in part through expanded negotiations with Syria and Iran. Seale is a journalist and the author of a number of books on the Middle East, including Asad of Syria: The Struggle for the Middle East.

As you read, consider the following questions:

1. According to the viewpoint, what were the two main recommendations from the Iraq Study Group?
2. What does the author contend was the result of Israel's 1982 invasion of Lebanon?
3. What does the author claim is the main reason that U.S. relations with Muslims have been "ruined?"

America is confronted in Iraq with one of its gravest crises since the Second World War. It has lost control of the situation. It is haemorrhaging men and treasure. It is facing if

Patrick Seale, "Is the Iraq War Linked to the Arab-Israeli Conflict?" *Gulf News*, December 15, 2006. Reproduced by permission.

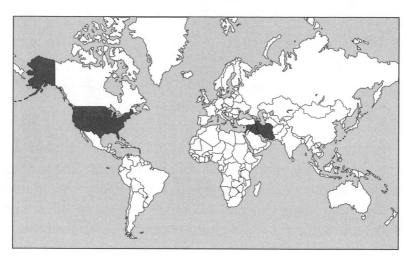

not defeat then utter failure. There is a sense in the US [United States] of an impending national catastrophe, reflected in President George W. Bush's collapsing approval ratings.

How can America extricate itself from a disastrous war which has strained its armed forces, sapped its finances and squandered its moral authority?

The Need for Iran and Syria to End the Conflict

The prescription offered by the high-level Iraq Study Group in its recent report [December 2006] is that US combat brigades should be withdrawn by early 2008 and that the US should engage in direct talks with Iran and Syria to secure their help in stabilising Iraq.

Above all, the underlying premise of the report is that the Iraq problem cannot be solved in isolation. It is linked, one way or another, to other major conflicts in the region with—at their heart—the unresolved problem of Israel's relations with its neighbours. A "comprehensive strategy" is required.

This is what James Baker and Lee Hamilton, co-chairmen of the Iraq Study Group, meant when they wrote: "The US will not be able to achieve its goals in the Middle East unless the US deals directly with the Arab-Israeli conflict."

This neocon camp rejects any notion of linkage between the savage war in Iraq and the Arab-Israeli conflict.

In the US, the report has sparked a huge national debate—indeed a battle royal—between America's old foreign policy establishment led by James Baker on the one hand and, on the other, the pro-Israeli neocons, backed by the Jewish lobby and right-wing think tanks—the very fanatics who captured America's Middle East policy under Bush's administration and were largely responsible for taking America into war.

This neocon camp rejects any notion of linkage between the savage war in Iraq and the Arab-Israeli conflict. This is because the one thing it fears is that the US might pressure Israel to withdraw from the Palestinian occupied territories and from Syria's Golan Heights in the context of a peace settlement.

And yet, the evidence of linkage between the various Middle East's conflicts is overwhelming. Would Iran's President Mahmoud Ahmadinejad have even conceived of staging the recent absurd and provocative conference questioning the Holocaust were it not for Israel's cruel oppression of the Palestinians? Would Ahmadinejad have a platform for his obnoxious ideas and wide support among Muslims were it not for Israel's destruction of what remains of Palestinian society by its targeted killings, expanding colonies, separation wall, bypass roads, checkpoints and all the inhuman machinery of military occupation?

Would Iran be so determined to master the uranium fuel cycle were it not for Israel's formidable arsenal of nuclear weapons, estimated by most experts to contain between 80 and 200 warheads? And are not Israel and its friends pressing the US to attack Iran's nuclear facilities?

The Link Between Iraq and the Arab-Israeli Conflict

Does linkage between Israel and the war in Iraq still need proving? Has it not been shown beyond dispute that it was concern for Israel's security—the wish to remove any threat to Israel from the east and the ambition to reshape the entire region in Israel's favour—that impelled deputy defence secretary Paul Wolfowitz and his colleague Douglas Feith to press ardently for war in Iraq?

For these pro-Israeli ideologues, invading Iraq and overthrowing Saddam Hussein was not enough. The country and its army had to be smashed beyond repair.

In his latest book, *State of Denial: Bush at War*, Bob Woodward, the celebrated US investigative journalist, makes clear that Paul Bremmer took two momentous decisions on his first full day as chief administrator in Baghdad. The first was to order the "De-Baathification of Iraqi Society", followed a day later by his Order Number 2, disbanding the Iraqi ministries of defence and interior, the entire Iraqi military and all of Saddam's bodyguard and special paramilitary organisations.

Syria needs to retain influence in Lebanon to prevent Israel or any other hostile power gaining a foothold there and mounting hostile operations against Syria from Lebanese soil.

Who instructed Bremmer to take these disastrous decisions, which have been largely responsible for the subsequent mess? The answer is Wolfowitz and Feith.

What about the crisis in Lebanon? Has Israel nothing to do with it? Hezbollah, the Shiite resistance movement, was created as a result of Israel's invasion of Lebanon in 1982 and its occupation of the south for the next 18 years. Without the invasion and occupation—without Israel's constant pressure on Lebanon since the 1960s and its repeated incursions—

The Iraq Study Group Recommendations on the Arab-Israeli Conflict

Given the ability of Iran and Syria to influence events within Iraq and their interest in avoiding chaos in Iraq, the United States should try to engage them constructively. In seeking to influence the behavior of both countries, the United States has disincentives and incentives available. Iran should stem the flow of arms and training to Iraq, respect Iraq's sovereignty and territorial integrity, and use its influence over Iraqi Shia groups to encourage national reconciliation. The issue of Iran's nuclear programs should continue to be dealt with by the five permanent members of the United Nations Security Council plus Germany. Syria should control its border with Iraq to stem the flow of funding, insurgents, and terrorists in and out of Iraq.

The United States cannot achieve its goals in the Middle East unless it deals directly with the Arab-Israeli conflict and regional instability. There must be a renewed and sustained commitment by the United States to a comprehensive Arab-Israeli peace on all fronts: Lebanon, Syria, and President Bush's June 2002 commitment to a two-state solution for Israel and Palestine. This commitment must include direct talks with, by, and between Israel, Lebanon, Palestinians (those who accept Israel's right to exist), and Syria.

Iraq Study Group, "The Iraq Study Group Report,"
December 6, 2006. www.usip.org.

there would have been no militant Shiite resurgence, no Hezbollah, and no challenge to Lebanon's delicate inter-confessional balance.

The present trial of strength in Lebanon between the Fouad Siniora government and pro-Syrian forces is largely to do with Syria's concern to retain a measure of influence in Beirut. But why is Syria so concerned with Lebanon? The two neighbours are, in any event, bound together by innumerable ties of family, of commerce and finance, of shared history, culture, language and ethnicity.

But there is another over-riding factor. It lies in the Arab-Israeli conflict of which Lebanon is a battleground.

Syria needs to retain influence in Lebanon to prevent Israel or any other hostile power gaining a foothold there and mounting hostile operations against Syria from Lebanese soil.

These are among the reasons why observers of the Middle East scene point to the obvious linkages between the various conflicts and insist that the unresolved Arab-Israeli conflict is the poison which has infected the whole region and ruined America's relations with Arabs and Muslims.

In recognition of this obvious fact, Baker and his colleagues called for "renewed and sustained commitment [by the United States] to a comprehensive Arab-Israeli peace on all fronts". Does the case still need to be argued?

The US Should Embrace the Iraq Study Group's Recommendations

Bush should heed Baker's advice in order to rescue his presidency and his own place in history. He should embrace the "comprehensive strategy" advocated by the Iraq Study Group. It is the only way, in the words of the report, "to restore America's standing and credibility in that part of the world".

Israel, too, should reflect on the damage the unresolved conflict is doing to its image in the world, to the health of its citizens and to its long-term security. According to most polls, some 65 per cent of Israelis—two thirds of the population—

are ready for peace with the Arabs on the basis of the land-for-peace formula enshrined in Security Council Resolutions 242 and 338.

What is Prime Minister Ehud Olmert waiting for? The way to disprove Ahmadinejad's prediction that Israel is heading for extinction is to make peace with the region and with the Palestinians in the first place—not to resort to force, and still less to reach for the nuclear button.

Resolving the Arab-Israeli Conflict Will Not End the Iraq War

Colin Rubenstein

In this viewpoint, the author Colin Rubenstein contends that the insurgency in Iraq and that country's Sunni versus Shiite strife is unrelated to the Arab-Israeli conflict. He asserts that even if Israel granted concessions to its Arab neighbors, peace and stability would not emerge in the region. Instead, countries such as Iran and Syria have used both the Iraq War and the Arab-Israeli conflict to pursue their own objectives. Colin Rubenstein is the executive director of the Australia/Israel and Jewish Affairs Council, and coauthor of Islam in Asia: Changing Political Realities.

As you read, consider the following questions:

1. Who does the author describe as the "realist" leader of the Iraq Survey Group?
2. According to the viewpoint, what country is endeavoring to gain control over the Middle East?
3. What does the viewpoint claim is the major hurdle for peace in the Arab-Israeli conflict?

The bipartisan Iraq Survey Group report to US [United States] President George Bush makes some reasonable if unsurprising recommendations about military strategy in

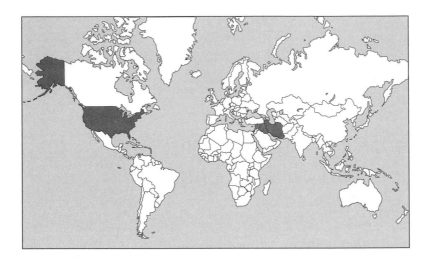

Iraq, but also two recommendations about wider Middle Eastern policy that are fundamentally flawed.

It says the Israel-Palestinian conflict is central to disorder in the Middle East, and calls for a new push to resolve it.

In fact, the recent history of the Middle East is filled with examples of conflicts that have nothing whatsoever to do with Israel—for instance the Shiite-Sunni confrontation in Iraq and Lebanon's political crisis between Hezbollah and the Siniora Government. The belief that forcing additional Israeli concessions will lead to the holy grail of Middle East peace is a dangerous pipedream based on misreading of the region's political map.

> *Iran, motivated both by Islamic messianism and Persian nationalism, is on a mission with its Syrian ally to gain hegemonic control of the Middle East, a goal that the leadership talks about quite openly.*

The Role of Iran and Syria

The group, under the leadership of the "realist" former US secretary of state James Baker, would also have us believe that

Iran and Syria can be induced to stop promoting sectarian violence in Iraq through positive "incentives" and high-level negotiations without preconditions. The logic behind this argument—that Iran and Syria have an interest in preventing the complete descent into chaos of neighbouring Iraq—is almost certainly wrong.

Iran, motivated both by Islamic messianism and Persian nationalism, is on a mission with its Syrian ally to gain hegemonic control of the Middle East, a goal that the leadership talks about quite openly. As long as the US is bogged down and Iraq is out of the Middle East equation, this serves their purposes.

Their price for any conceivable assistance in Iraq is likely to be prohibitive—assent to Iran's illegal nuclear weapons program, a blind eye to both states' support for terrorism, including sponsorship of a pro-Iranian regime in the Palestinian Authority, Syrian control over Lebanon restored, the return of the Golan Heights to Syria, and a right to a dominant Iranian-Syrian role in Iraq's future.

Well-intentioned outsiders, who adopt in principle the false rhetoric of the rejectionists that all the region's problems are connected with Israel, are helping to make them stronger and peace more remote.

This would effectively give Tehran the regional hegemonic role it is seeking, further radicalising the whole region as other players see the way the wind is blowing and jump on board.

Baker's view of the Israel-Palestinian peace process contains similar misperceptions. It has no significant effects on Iraq, and there are unfortunately few prospects of major progress towards a final resolution at the moment.

The problem is not that the Israelis refuse to concede a state to the Palestinians. It has been clear at least since Camp

---

Regime Change in Iraq

Israeli strategists generally believed that taking down the [Iraqi leader Saddam] Hussein regime could further upset an Iran-Iraq power balance that had already tilted in favour of Iran after the U.S. defeat of Hussein's army in the 1991 Gulf War. By 1996, however, neoconservatives with ties to the Likud Party were beginning to argue for a more aggressive joint U.S.-Israeli strategy aimed at a "rollback" of all of Israel's enemies in the region, including Iran, but beginning by taking down Hussein and putting a pro-Israeli regime in power there. . . .

Israel was more concerned with the relative military threat posed by Iran and Iraq, whereas neoconservatives in the Bush administration were focused on regime change in Iraq as a low-cost way of leveraging more ambitious changes in the region. From the neoconservative perspective, the very military weakness of Hussein's Iraq made it the logical target for the use of U.S. military power.

Gareth Porter, "Israel Warned US Not to Invade Iraq After 9/11," August 20, 2007. http://IPSNews.net.

David in 2000 that the Palestinians can have a state in the West Bank and Gaza any time that they are able and willing to offer peace in return. Even the traditionally hawkish former prime minister Ariel Sharon said as much on several occasions. Present Prime Minister Ehud Olmert was elected on a platform of essentially trying to give them that state even without such a commitment. What is holding peace back is not disagreement over scraps of land, but, primarily, the perpetuation of Arab and Islamist rejectionism of Israel in any borders.

Hamas and Regional Strife

And unfortunately, the Hamas Government of the Palestinian Authority is clearly part of the rejectionist trend across the region led by Tehran and Damascus. As Palestinian academic expert Mustafa Assawaf recently said, Hamas would never recognise Israel "even if the temptation was world recognition and a (Palestinian) state". The Fatah movement of President Mahmoud Abbas might conceivably cut a deal, but it is in disarray, and there is no possibility it can deliver on a peace agreement.

Hamas has indicated it might agree to a temporary truce in exchange for not only every centimetre of the West Bank (they already have all of Gaza), but also the fulfilment of a legally baseless "Palestinian right of return" to Israel that is a formula to destroy Israel demographically. A deal on these terms is not possible from any Israeli point of view.

Islamist terror is based on a totalitarian Islamist ideology. Solving the Arab-Israel conflict, even if achievable, would do nothing to eliminate the economic and political deficiencies in the Arab states that make this ideology popular and were highlighted in the UN's [United Nations] Arab Human Development Report of 2002.

Moreover, Islamic extremists and those susceptible to their message would actually view an Israel-Palestinian two-state resolution as an additional grievance—the West forcing Palestinians to accept Israel's so-called theft of their land.

Well-intentioned outsiders, who adopt in principle the false rhetoric of the rejectionists that all the region's problems are connected with Israel, are helping to make them stronger and peace more remote.

Peace, when it comes, will be a great blessing to Israel and to the Palestinians, and will gladden people of goodwill around the world. It is therefore a terrible mistake to allow eagerness for peace to cause us to ignore the prerequisites for its achievement.

The Ongoing Conflicts in Iraq and Israel Should Be Resolved by the Arab League

Richard Seymour

In this viewpoint, Richard Seymour contends that the Arab League, potentially the most influential organization in the Middle East, has been largely underutilized in addressing conflicts in Iraq or surrounding Israel. He explores the problems that have constrained the League, including past divisions between pro-American and pro-Soviet nations and the current divide between Sunni and Shiite nations. Seymour also explores possible steps that could be taken to enhance the organization's role in fostering peace. Seymour is an author who lives in London and frequently writes about the Middle East.

As you read, consider the following questions:

1. What does the viewpoint declare is the most notable challenge confronted by the Arab League?

2. How many companies were boycotted by the League during the height of its boycott against Israel?

3. On the eve of the Iraq War, what did the Arab League vote to do?

Richard Seymour, "Strength in Numbers: The Arab League, a Toothless Tiger or the Region's Last Hope for Equanimity and Equilibrium?" *The Middle East*, November 2006, pp. 26–29. Copyright © IC Publications 2006. Reproduced by permission.

Everyone, it seems, has a solution to the current crises in the Middle East, whether it's the earnest diplomats of the UN [United Nations], meeting on occasions too numerous to document to discuss Iraq, Iran, Israel, the Palestinians, Lebanon, and Syria, or the bureaucrats of the European Union (EU), with their own plans for peace and stability in this, the hub of civilisation for millennia. It seems the rest of the world is convinced the Middle East is either unwilling or simply incapable of putting its own house in order.

Formation of the Arab League

Yet amid the various groups jostling for prominence, the League of Arab Nations or, as it is more commonly known, the Arab League, has been largely ignored. The Arab League was formed in 1945 when Egypt, Lebanon, Jordan, Syria, Saudi Arabia, Yemen and Iraq, plus a representative of the Palestinian Arabs, joined together in a bid to forge a common political path. That membership has since swelled to include such countries as Kuwait, Sudan, Algeria and others across the Arab world.

The League has faced many challenges over more than 60 years, most notably the Arab/Israeli conflict: in 1948, when six of the League's members (Iraq, Egypt, Jordan, Saudi Arabia, Lebanon and Syria) launched a military offensive against the newly proclaimed state of Israel.

[The Arab League] has established the Arab Common Market, the Arab Financial Organisation and telecommunication postal unions.

The Arab League and the Arab-Israeli Conflict

Publicly united in the aim of fighting Israel, privately the coalition began to fragment with the suspicion that some were using the attack as a means to consolidate their own positions, and the operation failed. In the decades that have followed, the Arab League has failed to make real progress regarding the plight of the Palestinian people.

But the remit of the Arab League goes far beyond the Israeli/Palestinian conflict. Its main aim is to organise the economic and business affairs of the region. To this end it has established the Arab Common Market, the Arab Financial Organisation and telecommunication and postal unions.

Accomplishments of the League

It has also furthered Arab culture by means of education and the restoration and preservation of Arab heritage. But perhaps one of its most successful campaigns was the coordinated boycott by all Arab nations of companies involved in doing business with Israel. At its height, the campaign saw more than 8,000 companies ruled out of trading with the Arab world.

What makes the Arab League almost unique, and what could provide a great source of its strength, is that it is based largely on culture and not, like the EU, to use one example, on geography. While Europe struggles to unite its traditionally disunited member states behind a common goal, the Arab League states, by definition, should come to the table with much common ground between them.

That is the theory, anyway. In practice, differences between member states have hampered the effectiveness of the League to the point where many are beginning to suggest that it is time the organisation was disbanded.

The League has made it possible for Arab governments to share information and coordinate policies more freely since its inception, but it is also true that similar freedoms are not enjoyed by the populations of all member states, some of whom still suffer oppression, poverty and instability.

Problems of the League

A recent public debate in Doha voted in favour of disbanding the League, its opponents claiming it to be weak and useless. Those in favour of maintaining it argued that while not without problems, it was still the only common thread that bound the Arab world together; however, even they concede it needs considerable reform to survive and be effective.

One problem facing the Arab League—the one its opponents say dooms it to certain failure—is the tension that exists between individual Arab states over various issues. It is said that member states will never be able to agree on anything really worthwhile, so long as each looks only to protect its own interests at the expense of others.

Disbanding the League would not see those differences and self-interests evaporate. Maintaining the League is not, however, enough to ensure that, eventually, the Arab world will fall into line behind a single vision.

The League vs. the European Union

While Europe is today a largely peaceful and stable continent, the EU was born out of war and mutual distrust. The first step was to lay down an economic plan that would be to the benefit of each member state. It soon became apparent that the prosperity of one's former enemies was essential for one's own long term well-being.

In a perfect example of this, Britain donated billions of pounds to Spain in a bid to boost its economy. This was, quite naturally, criticised by many in Britain who felt the money would be better spent boosting the British economy. But now, Spain is one of the most economically progressive countries in Europe and Britain has made its investment back, and much more besides, in trade with the southern European country.

And now with a common currency and a single, Europe-wide interest rate, it is more essential than ever that once-bickering governments agree [to] common policies as efficiently as possible. A natural consequence of this has been greater cooperation on all areas of European life including policing, justice, civil rights, and even, tentatively, foreign policy.

Currently, the [Arab League] is 'toothless'. It has little power to enforce agreements and none at all unless a unanimous decision is reached.

If the same is to be achieved with the Arab League, first its member states must want it to work. There is an apparent lack of enthusiasm among some members that must be overcome if they are to be galvanised into an effective region-wide socio-political force.

The need for this was highlighted earlier this year [2006] when the UN demanded in a resolution that Syria recognise the sovereignty and territorial integrity of its neighbour, Lebanon. Syria is a founding member of the Arab League, which includes in its charter that its members respect the sovereignty and territorial integrity of its neighbours. In other words, if the charter were worth the paper it was written on, Syria should not have needed to be told.

Currently, the organisation is 'toothless'. It has little power to enforce agreements and none at all unless a unanimous decision is reached, which, at the very best of times, is unlikely.

The League and Iraq

The current instability in the region is a compelling example of why the Arab League should work on developing its muscle. The problem of Saddam Hussein was never addressed effectively and it did not go away on its own. As a result, an American-led coalition took control of the situation.

Prior to the start of the latest Iraq conflict, the Arab League voted in favour of continuing the weapons inspections, expressing the fear that war would see Iraq break apart, leading to instability spreading throughout the region.

Members of the Arab League and Year of Membership

Algeria	1962
Bahrain	1971
Comoros	1993
Djibouti	1977
Egypt	1945
Iraq	1945
Jordan	1945
Kuwait	1961
Lebanon	1945
Libya	1953
Mauritania	1973
Morocco	1958
Oman	1971
Palestine	1976
Qatar	1971
Saudi Arabia	1945
Somalia	1974
Sudan	1956
Syria	1945
Tunisia	1958
United Arab Emirates	1972
Yemen	1945

Compiled by the editor.

Critics of this stance claimed League members were only concerned that once Saddam Hussein fell, one of them would be next. This may have been true, but it is an unavoidable fact that had they had their way, weapons inspectors would have been able to declare what even Washington has been forced to admit—Saddam Hussein had no weapons of mass destruction.

Unfortunately, the Arab League either failed to act soon enough or firmly enough and, when it came to the moment of truth, the rest of the world showed complete disregard for its concerns. But when a weekend-long meeting of League members failed even to set a date for the problem to be discussed, that is hardly a surprise.

If the Arab League is going to be able to continue as a legitimate organisation, its members must decide to abide by its charter and to give themselves greater power to see it enforced.

If the threat of the instability in Iraq spreading further afield has shaken Arab governments, then perhaps this is the moment the Arab League will finally sort itself out. But even this is problematic. Whereas, in the past, the League was split along the lines of who was pro-American and who was pro-Soviet, there now exist fissures separating the more moderate states from the others.

There are also suspicions, expressed by the Shi'a Iraqi government, that the mostly Sunni Arab League has been reluctant to help as it takes its first, faltering steps into the post-Saddam era. However, the League has shown willingness in recent months to play a more active role in the reconstruction of Iraq.

Challenges of the League

If the Arab League is going to be able to continue as a legitimate organisation, its members must decide to abide by its charter and to give themselves greater power to see it enforced. They will have to overcome the fears, still rife in Europe over the same issue, that this will see sovereignty devolved.

But when a foreign army can roll into the Arab region at will, having failed to secure the assent of its member states, then sovereignty starts to mean very little. The supreme authority to govern oneself can only be maintained in the Arab world in the current climate if its governments unite and become stronger than the sum of their parts. And the supreme authority to govern oneself is, after all, what sovereignty is all about.

The United States Invaded Iraq to Protect Israel

Emad Mekay

In the viewpoint below, Emad Mekay reports on comments made by a senior advisor to the George W. Bush administration who suggested that the United States went to war with Iraq to improve Israel's security. The author asserts that the Bush administration had a number of pro-Israeli members who viewed the conflict with Iraq as part of a larger strategy in the Middle East to enhance the security of Israel, a staunch ally of the United States. Mekay is the trade and finance reporter for Inter Press Service News Agency in Washington, D.C.

As you read, consider the following questions:

1. According to the viewpoint, what does the Bush administration claim are the three reasons it went to war with Iraq?

2. What is the President's Foreign Intelligence Advisory Board?

3. According to Mekay, why does Hamas want biological weapons?

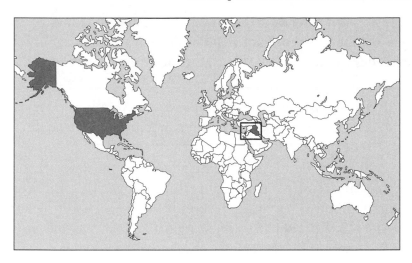

Iraq under Saddam Hussein did not pose a threat to the United States but it did to Israel, which is one reason why Washington invaded the Arab country, according to a speech made by a member of a top-level White House intelligence group.

Philip Zelikow's Remarks

IPS [Inter Press Service News Agency] uncovered the remarks by Philip Zelikow, who is now the executive director of the body set up to investigate the terrorist attacks on the United States in September 2001—the 9/11 Commission—in which he suggests a prime motive for the invasion just over one year ago [2003] was to eliminate a threat to Israel, a staunch U.S. ally in the Middle East.

Zelikow's casting of the attack on Iraq as one launched to protect Israel appears at odds with the public position of President George W. Bush and his administration, which has never overtly drawn the link between its war on the regime of former president [Saddam] Hussein and its concern for Israel's security.

The administration has instead insisted it launched the war to liberate the Iraqi people, destroy Iraq's weapons of mass destruction (WMD) and to protect the United States.

Israel is Washington's biggest ally in the Middle East, receiving annual direct aid of three to four billion dollars.

Zelikow made his statements about "the unstated threat" during his tenure on a highly knowledgeable and well-connected body known as the President's Foreign Intelligence Advisory Board (PFIAB), which reports directly to the president. He served on the board between 2001 and 2003.

"Why would Iraq attack America or use nuclear weapons against us? I'll tell you what I think the real threat (is) and actually has been since 1990—it's the threat against Israel," Zelikow told a crowd at the University of Virginia on Sep. 10, 2002, speaking on a panel of foreign policy experts assessing the impact of 9/11 and the future of the war on the al-Qaeda terrorist organisation.

"And this is the threat that dare not speak its name, because the Europeans don't care deeply about that threat, I will tell you frankly. And the American government doesn't want to lean too hard on it rhetorically, because it is not a popular sell," said Zelikow.

The statements are the first to surface from a source closely linked to the Bush administration acknowledging that the war, which has so far [as of March 2004] cost the lives of nearly 600 U.S. troops and thousands of Iraqis, was motivated by Washington's desire to defend the Jewish state.

The administration, which is surrounded by staunch pro-Israel, neo-conservative hawks, is currently fighting an extensive campaign to ward off accusations that it derailed the "war on terrorism" it launched after 9/11 by taking a detour to Iraq, which appears to have posed no direct threat to the United States.

Israel is Washington's biggest ally in the Middle East, receiving annual direct aid of three to four billion dollars.

Ties to the Bush Administration

Even though members of the 16-person PFIAB come from outside government, they enjoy the confidence of the president and have access to all information related to foreign intelligence that they need to play their vital advisory role.

Known in intelligence circles as "Piffy-ab", the board is supposed to evaluate the nation's intelligence agencies and probe any mistakes they make. The unpaid appointees on the board require a security clearance known as "code word" that is higher than top secret.

The national security adviser to former President George H.W. Bush (1989–93), Brent Scowcroft, currently chairs the board in its work overseeing a number of intelligence bodies, including the Central Intelligence Agency (CIA), the various military intelligence groups and the Pentagon's National Reconnaissance Office. . . .

Zelikow has long-established ties to the Bush administration. Before his appointment to PFIAB in October 2001, he was part of the current president's transition team in January 2001.

In that capacity, Zelikow drafted a memo for National Security Adviser Condoleezza Rice on reorganising and restructuring the National Security Council (NSC) and prioritising its work.

Richard A. Clarke, who was counter-terrorism coordinator for Bush's predecessor President Bill Clinton (1993–2001), also worked for Bush senior, and has recently accused the current administration of not heeding his terrorism warnings, said Zelikow was among those he briefed about the urgent threat from al-Qaeda in December 2000.

The Iraq War Was Fought for Israel

Why did the United States attack Iraq?

Whatever the secondary reasons for the war, the crucial factor in President Bush's decision to attack was to help Israel. With support from Israel and America's Jewish-Zionist lobby, and prodded by Jewish "neo-conservatives" holding high-level positions in his administration, President Bush—who was already fervently committed to Israel—resolved to invade and subdue one of Israel's chief regional enemies.

This is so widely understood in Washington that US Senator Ernest Hollings was moved in May 2004 to acknowledge that the US invaded Iraq "to secure Israel," and "everybody" knows it. He also identified three of the influential pro-Israel Jews in Washington who played an important role in prodding the US into war: Richard Perle, chair of the Pentagon's Defense Policy Board; Paul Wolfowitz, Deputy Defense Secretary; and Charles Krauthammer, columnist and author.

Hollings referred to the cowardly reluctance of his Congressional colleagues to acknowledge this truth openly, saying that "nobody is willing to stand up and say what is going on." Due to "the pressures we get politically," he added, members of Congress uncritically support Israel and its policies.

Mark Weber, "Iraq! A War for Israel,"
March 2008. www.ihr.org.

Rice herself had served in the NSC during the first Bush administration, and subsequently teamed up with Zelikow on a 1995 book about the unification of Germany.

Zelikow had ties with another senior Bush administration official—Robert Zoellick, the current trade representative. The two wrote three books together, including one in 1998 on the United States and the "Muslim Middle East".

Aside from his position at the 9/11 commission, Zelikow is now also director of the Miller Centre of Public Affairs and White Burkett Miller Professor of History at the University of Virginia.

His close ties to the administration prompted accusations of a conflict of interest in 2002 from families of victims of the 9/11 attacks, who protested his appointment to the investigative body.

Saddam's Threat to Israel

In his university speech, Zelikow, who strongly backed attacking the Iraqi dictator, also explained the threat to Israel by arguing that Baghdad was preparing in 1990–91 to spend huge amounts of "scarce hard currency" to harness "communications against electromagnetic pulse", a side-effect of a nuclear explosion that could sever radio, electronic and electrical communications.

[Professor Nathan Brown] downplayed the Israel link. 'In terms of securing Israel, it doesn't make sense to me because the Israelis are probably more concerned about Iran than they were about Iraq in terms of the long-term strategic threat.'

That was "a perfectly absurd expenditure unless you were going to ride out a nuclear exchange—they (Iraqi officials) were not preparing to ride out a nuclear exchange with us. Those were preparations to ride out a nuclear exchange with the Israelis", according to Zelikow.

He also suggested that the danger of biological weapons falling into the hands of the anti-Israeli Islamic Resistance

Movement, known by its Arabic acronym Hamas, would threaten Israel rather than the United States, and that those weapons could have been developed to the point where they could deter Washington from attacking Hamas.

"Play out those scenarios," he told his audience, "and I will tell you, people have thought about that, but they are just not talking very much about it".

"Don't look at the links between Iraq and al-Qaeda, but then ask yourself the question, 'gee, is Iraq tied to Hamas and the Palestinian Islamic Jihad and the people who are carrying out suicide bombings in Israel'? Easy question to answer; the evidence is abundant."

To date, the possibility of the United States attacking Iraq to protect Israel has been only timidly raised by some intellectuals and writers, with few public acknowledgements from sources close to the administration.

Analysts who reviewed Zelikow's statements said they are concrete evidence of one factor in the rationale for going to war, which has been hushed up.

"Those of us speaking about it sort of routinely referred to the protection of Israel as a component," said Phyllis Bennis of the Washington-based Institute of Policy Studies. "But this is a very good piece of evidence of that."

Others say the administration should be blamed for not making known to the public its true intentions and real motives for invading Iraq.

"They (the administration) made a decision to invade Iraq, and then started to search for a policy to justify it. It was a decision in search of a policy and because of the odd way they went about it, people are trying to read something into it," said Nathan Brown, professor of political science at George Washington University and an expert on the Middle East.

But he downplayed the Israel link. "In terms of securing Israel, it doesn't make sense to me because the Israelis are probably more concerned about Iran than they were about Iraq in terms of the long-term strategic threat," he said.

Still, Brown says Zelikow's words carried weight.

"Certainly his position would allow him to speak with a little bit more expertise about the thinking of the Bush administration, but it doesn't strike me that he is any more authoritative than [former Deputy Secretary of Defense Paul] Wolfowitz, or Rice or [former Secretary of State Colin] Powell or anybody else. All of them were sort of fishing about for justification for a decision that has already been made," Brown said.

Israel's Influence in Launching the Iraq War Is Often Overstated

Dore Gold

In the following viewpoint, the author, Dore Gold, examines why Israel's influence in initiating the Iraq War has often been overstated. He asserts that the war actually created new threats to Israel. Gold explains that there were more serious security threats to Israel than Iraq, particularly Syria and Iran. He concludes by exploring the common interests shared by Israel and the United States. Dore Gold is the author of Hatred's Kingdom: How Saudi Arabia Supports the New Global Terrorism *and the president of the Jerusalem Center for Public Affairs.*

As you read, consider the following questions:

1. What enemy countries are identified as part of Israel's "Eastern Front" in the viewpoint?

2. What advantages did Iran have over Iraq in the quest to develop nuclear weapons?

3. According to the viewpoint, what is Richard Clarke's thesis about the dominant consideration in going to war with Iraq?

Dore Gold, "Wartime Witch Hunt: Blaming Israel for the Iraq War," *Jerusalem Issue Briefs*, vol. 3, no. 25, June 3, 2004. www.jcpa.org. Reproduced by permission.

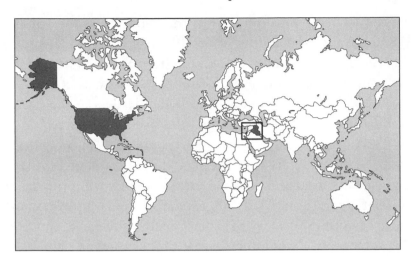

An insidious but steady drumbeat can be discerned over the last several weeks that seeks to link Israel with the U.S. decision to launch the Iraq War. Back in 2003, it was Yasser Arafat who charged that the Israeli government was "the first inciter for the war against Iraq." About the same time, Patrick Buchanan charged in his *American Conservative* magazine that "a cabal of polemicists and public officials seek to ensnare our country in a series of wars that are not in America's interests." He went on to blame them for "colluding with Israel to ignite those wars."

On the liberal side, Chris Matthews, who hosts MSNBC's *Hardball*, echoed Buchanan when he spoke about "conservative people out there, some of them Jewish . . . who believe that if we don't fight Iraq, Israel will be in danger." Likewise, former Democratic presidential candidate [in 1984 and 1988 elections] Gary Hart warned of "ideologues" who were not able to distinguish between their loyalty "to their original homelands" and loyalty "to America and its national interests."

A New Wave of Scapegoating

The newest wave in 2004 is often more subtle but also far more mainstream. Thus, in May 2004, CBS's *60 Minutes* interviewed General Anthony Zinni, former commander of the U.S. Central Command, who blasted the civilian leadership in the Pentagon for faulty strategy in Iraq. Steve Kroft of CBS then added fuel to the fire of Zinni's attack by asserting that the neo-conservatives among the civilian leaders in the Pentagon had an agenda to "strengthen the position of Israel."

Of course, what has given these comments saliency in the media is the difficulty the U.S. Army has encountered in dealing with the insurgency in Iraq after the completion of major combat operations. Had this aspect of the Iraq War gone more smoothly, as was perhaps originally anticipated, much of this scapegoating would not have even been voiced.

But it continued nonetheless. *Newsweek* reminded its readers in a May 31 [2004] cover-story on Ahmad Chalabi, the Iraqi National Congress leader whose offices were recently raided by Iraqi and U.S. security personnel, of how he had previously become a favorite of the Pentagon elite: Chalabi spoke in 1997 at the Jewish Institute for National Security Affairs (JINSA), *Newsweek* emphasized, adding that in private conversations Chalabi assured his neo-conservative friends that a post-Saddam [Hussein] Iraq "would be an Arab country friendly to Israel." A few weeks earlier, Senator Ernest "Fritz" Hollings (D-S.C.) wrote in a Charleston newspaper that behind the U.S. decision to go to war against Saddam Hussein was "President Bush's policy to secure Israel." Rather than retract his language, Hollings reiterated his claims later on the floor of the U.S. Senate.

The main charge by the current detractors of Israel is that the primary *interest of the Bush administration in going to war against Saddam Hussein was to defend Israeli security interests.*

The main charge by the current detractors of Israel is that the *primary* interest of the Bush administration in going to

Recent U.S. Aid to Israel *(millions of dollars)*					
Year	Total	Military Grant	Economic Grant	Immig. Grant	American Schools and Hospitals Abroad (ASHA)	All other
1949–1996	68,030.9	29,014.9	23,122.4	868.9	121.4	14,903.3
1997	3,132.1	1,800.0	1,200.0	80.0	2.1	50.0
1998	3,080.0	1,800.0	1,200.0	80.0	—	—
1999	3,010.0	1,860.0	1,080.0	70.0	—	—
2000	4,131.85	3,120.0	949.1	60.0	2.75	—
2001	2,876.05	1,975.6	838.2	60.0	2.25	—
2002	2,850.65	2,040.0	720.0	60.0	2.65	28.0
2003	3,745.15	3,086.4	596.1	59.6	3.05	—
2004	2,687.25	2,147.3	477.2	49.7	3.15	9.9
2005	2,612.15	2,202.2	357.0	50.0	2.95	—
2006	2,534.5	2,257.0	237.0	40.0	—	0.5
2007	2,500.2	2,340.0	120.0	40.0	—	0.2
Total	101,190.8	53,643.4	30,897.0	1,518.2	140.3	14,991.9

TAKEN FROM: Jeremy M. Sharp, "U.S. Foreign Aid to Israel," Congressional Research Service, January 2, 2008. http//asserts.openers.com.

war against Saddam Hussein was to defend Israeli security interests. Bush critic Richard Clarke, who previously served in the administration, also mentions the Israel factor as one of five rationales of the Bush administration for the Iraq War, but at least he sets it aside as a *main* consideration, preferring instead to focus on the concern with finding a long-term alternative to Saudi Arabian oil. Another variation on the Israel theme is the assertion made by Nicholas Kristof, the *New York Times* columnist, that General Zinni heard from administration officials that the Iraq War would advance the Israeli-Palestinian peace process because "the road to Jerusalem leads through Baghdad." According to this thesis, the Iraq War would chiefly help Israel's drive to obtain peace on reasonable terms—still a benefit to Israel.

For critics of President Bush in the heat of an election year, who reject the notion that the Iraq War was fought over weapons of mass destruction, the war on terrorism, or over human rights and a promise of a democratic Iraq, the Israel factor is a useful instrument for bashing the administration by ascribing the war to alien considerations having nothing to do with U.S. interests.

The Israeli Interest in the Iraq War

Iraq is one of several Arab countries that have in the past constituted Israel's "Eastern Front." Historically, they include Syria, Jordan, Iraq, and Saudi Arabia. But whereas Syria devoted almost its entire ground order-of-battle to wars with Israel, Iraq sent only expeditionary forces that never exceeded one-third of its total army in 1948, 1967, and 1973. In the past, the Iraqi military reserved most of its units for internal threats (such as against the Kurdish militia) or for threats from Iran. Moreover, Iraq is not contiguous with Israel, as is Syria, and hence required the permission of third parties to project its military forces across 300 miles to reach Israel on the ground.

In short, the Iraqi threat against Israel could be substantial if Iraq maintained a 40-division army as it did prior to its invasion of Kuwait and the 1991 Gulf War, when in theory it could have threatened Israel with a 12-division force. However, by 2003, the Iraqi Army had been severely degraded in both military manpower and equipment. Continuing UN [United Nations] sanctions made Iraqi re-armament difficult. Thus, Iraq was clearly not Israel's primary concern.

The Israel factor is a useful instrument for bashing the administration by ascribing the war to alien considerations having nothing to do with U.S. interests.

What about missiles and weapons of mass destruction in Iraq? Looking at publicized Israeli preparations and statements before and after the Iraq War, it is clear that Israeli officials were concerned with this aspect of Iraqi military power, but not overwhelmingly so. The Head of Military Intelligence of the Israel Defense Forces, Maj.-Gen. Aharon Zeevi-Farkash, told the Israeli daily *Yediot Ahronot* that Iraq maintained a "residual capability" after 1998 that included "tens of missiles and several chemical and biological warheads." Analyzing the prewar training patterns of the Iraqi Air Force, there were concerns in Israel that Baghdad sought to prepare long-range attack options, but these were not necessarily Israel-specific.

The Threat from Syria

By contrast, in early 2003, among Israel's neighbors, Syria possessed by far the largest stockpile of ballistic missiles—at least 500 missiles or about ten times the size of the Iraqi arsenal. The Syrians could mount on them the same biological or chemical warheads as the Iraqis, with one important difference: Iraq had to reduce the size of its warheads in order to extend the range of its missiles; thus, the quantities of non-conventional material that could be delivered by the Syrian missile forces was considerably greater.

Speaking in August 2002, Israel's former defense minister, Moshe Arens, concluded that in the immediate future, "the [missile] threat that Israel most likely will have to contend with" is that of Syria. He described the Iraqi capability as "relatively limited." During the same month, Israel's current chief of staff, Lt. Gen. Moshe Ya'alon, declared in Jerusalem that the threat posed by Iraq "doesn't make me lose sleep." In an open address at the Jaffee Center for Strategic Studies in October 2002, the former head of analysis for Israeli Military Intelligence, Maj.-Gen. (res.) Yaakov Amidror, explained to an Israeli audience that since the Iraqi missile units had not conducted military exercises and lacked spare parts, the Iraqi threat to Israel was minimal.

In other words, the American war against Iraq may have had an unintended side-effect of removing a secondary or tertiary threat to Israel, but *not* a primary threat. For other states in the region, like Iran, Kuwait, and Saudi Arabia, whose territory was actually invaded or threatened by Iraqi forces in the last 20 years, Iraq posed a potential primary threat. Indeed, when one considers the fact that Saddam Hussein's military killed hundreds of thousands of Muslims in successive wars with Iran, the Kurds, Iraqi Shiites, and Kuwaitis, while perhaps one Israeli was killed due to the Iraqi missile attack on Israel in 1991, the theory that the Bush administration fought Iraq on behalf of Israel looks especially ludicrous. And while Iraq supported Palestinian terrorism against Israel over the last number of years, it was only a minor financial sponsor compared to Iran and Saudi Arabia.

The American war against Iraq may have had an unintended side-effect of removing a secondary or tertiary threat to Israel, but not a primary threat.

Risks Israel Undertook Because of the Iraq War

If Israel played down the Iraqi threat prior to 2003, once the countdown to the U.S.-UK-led campaign got underway, the Israeli government had to undertake serious civil-defense preparations. The most notable development was a sudden nationwide effort to distribute gas masks and nerve gas antidote. It was assumed that Iraq could not retaliate against Washington or London, which were beyond the range of its missiles, but Baghdad might strike out against U.S. regional allies like Israel. As a result, Israel had to prepare itself to absorb this sort of Iraqi counterattack which, if not for the coalition's war on Iraq, was unlikely to have been directed against Israel like a bolt out of the blue. In other words, while Israel clearly benefited from the removal of a secondary or tertiary threat to its security, from its perspective, Israel assumed tremendous risks in the process.

For regardless of what happened to Iraq's weapons of mass destruction, Israeli military intelligence had little doubt that a small amount of this weaponry was still retained by Saddam Hussein, enough to cause great harm to a small country. Moreover, Israel's concerns with a potential biological weapons attack included contagious diseases, like smallpox. Indeed, Israeli health workers were vaccinated for smallpox as an additional prewar precaution.

How would Saddam Hussein deliver these weapons over Israel, given the small size of the Iraqi missile force? The Knesset Foreign Affairs and Defense Committee's investigation of Israel's wartime intelligence on Iraq disclosed that the Israeli military discerned long-range Iraqi Air Force exercises before the war that also included the use of pilotless drone aircraft.

The use of suicide terrorists could not be dismissed either. While the extent of the al-Qaeda/Saddam link is a matter of dispute in the U.S., there is no question that the Palestine Liberation Front (PLF) of Abul Abbas operated out of Baghdad and his operatives were trained by Iraqi intelligence. This relatively small organization, which was a component of the PLO [Palestine Liberation Organization], had dispatched operatives from Iraq to the West Bank before and could have been the vehicle for delivering such weapons, in coordination with larger Palestinian groups such as Fatah-Tanzim or Hamas. Indeed, these groups had experimented, on a limited scale and without much success, with suicide bombs that were tainted with biological weapons components. In short, it would have been foolhardy for Israel to dismiss out of hand the possibility of Iraqi retaliation in response to the coalition attack on Iraq.

If Israel wanted to get into the business—which it did not—of prodding the U.S. to go to war on its behalf, it would have chosen Iran and not Iraq.

Iran Is the Real Long-Term Threat to Israel

If prior to the Iraq War the Israeli security establishment was somewhat ambivalent about the extent of the Iraqi threat, there was one state that threatened Israel about which Israeli statements were unmistakably clear: Iran. Israel used language with respect to Iran that it never used regarding Iraq. Thus, in 2004 Prime Minister Ariel Sharon would call Iran "the main existential threat to Israel." Arriving in Washington a few weeks after the September 11, 2001, attack, former Deputy Defense Minister Ephraim Sneh told reporters: "Iran stands in first place as a sponsor of terrorism." Clearly, if Israel wanted to get into the business—which it did not—of prodding the U.S. to go to war on its behalf, it would have chosen Iran and not Iraq.

Why was the Iranian threat worse than the Iraqi threat? Despite the removal of UN monitors from Iraq in 1998, Iraq, nonetheless, had been under international inspection for more than a decade, limiting the progress of its clandestine programs in developing prohibited weapons under UN Security Council Resolution 687. Iran did not face the same international constraints, so both its nuclear and ballistic missile programs were far more advanced. For example, the bipartisan, congressionally-mandated Rumsfeld Commission Report of 1998 predicted that Iran could put together an intercontinental-range missile within five years from making the decision, while Iraq would need double that time.

While Iran was completing the development of its 1,300-kilometer-range Shihab-III missile, it had already placed thousands of Fajr artillery rockets in Lebanon that could strike central Israel. These forward-deployed rocket systems were under Iranian command and control. Iraq had no equivalent territory along Israel's borders that it could exploit in order to threaten Israeli cities.

On the nuclear side as well, Iran was moving ahead of Iraq by the year 2000. Speaking in Jerusalem in July 2000, former UNSCOM [United Nations Special Commission] executive-chairman Richard Butler disclosed that, while the Iraqi design for producing nuclear weapons was advanced, Baghdad did not possess the necessary enriched uranium or plutonium for producing an atomic weapon. Yet Iran possessed what Iraq lacked. The International Atomic Energy Agency (IAEA) already knew about Iran's covert nuclear enrichment facility at Natanz by September 2002 when the issue was raised by IAEA Director General Dr. Mohammed ElBaradei with Iran's vice-president. A confidential IAEA report in 2003 described how the clandestine Iranian nuclear enrichment program had been based on complex technologies developed over the past 18 years. Thus, Israel would have had good reasons to be more concerned about Iran than about Iraq prior to the Iraq War. . . .

Common Interests of the U.S. and Israel

What is . . . disturbing about the effort to blame Israel for the Iraq War is the accompanying tendency to reject the notion that the U.S. and Israel are both allies with joint interests. Because Winston Churchill met with President [Franklin Delano] Roosevelt before Pearl Harbor to discuss the joint interests of Britain and the U.S., does that mean that the British dragged the U.S. into the Second World War? The 9/11 attacks on New York and Washington have only enlarged the scope of the joint interests of the U.S. and Israel to defeat global terrorist organizations that are harbored by rogue regimes in the Middle East. If Israel didn't exist, that would remain a primary U.S. interest today.

Why did the U.S. go to war against Iraq? The declarations of the Bush administration are well-known regarding weapons of mass destruction and the war on terrorism. But wars are launched for multiple reasons, many of which are not always pronounced. The U.S. was attacked by the Japanese in 1941, but nonetheless decided on a "Europe-First" strategy to eliminate Nazi Germany, for Hitler's hegemony over all of Europe was the greater threat. There is something persuasive about Richard Clarke's thesis that in the case of Iraq, the dominant consideration was concern over the long-term stability of the

House of Saud and the need for the U.S. to replace a shaky Saudi Arabia with an alternative friendly source of oil for the industrial West. Considering the widespread presence of al-Qaeda cells across virtually all parts of Saudi Arabia that now has become evident from repeated terrorist attacks during 2003/4, this American consideration has been proven to be prescient. But this has absolutely nothing to do with Israel.

Yet, many neo-isolationist critics of the Iraq War do not understand why America is fighting wars all of a sudden in the distant Middle East. Partly for that reason, they think America's war on terrorism was caused by considerations related to Israel. During most of the twentieth century, the main threats to U.S. national security emanated from the European continent, evidenced by the decisions of past American administrations to enter World War I, World War II, and to extend the U.S. military umbrella over Europe during the Cold War.

Given the global pattern of non-conventional weapons proliferation, the spread of long-range delivery systems, and the sources of the current wave of international terrorism, the Middle East has replaced Europe as the region that poses the greatest threat to the American heartland. That fact has nothing to do with the purported lobbying efforts of a group of American citizens who have been singled out by irresponsible commentators. In the late 1930s, a group of racists charged Roosevelt, the British, and the Jews with forcing America into war. Their intellectual offspring are doing the same 70 years later.

Periodical Bibliography

The following articles have been selected to supplement the diverse views presented in this chapter.

Max Abrahms "A Window of Opportunity for Israel?" *Middle East Quarterly*, Summer 2003.

Spencer Ackerman "Iraq'd," *The New Republic*, October 11, 2004.

Gawdat Bahgat "Israel and Iran in the New Middle East," *Contemporary Security Policy*, December 2006.

Nomi Bar-Yaacov "New Imperatives for Israeli-Palestinian Peace," *Survival*, Summer 2003.

Zbigniew Brzezinski "Lowered Vision," *New Republic*, June 7, 2004.

The Economist "Fumbling the Moment," May 29, 2004.

James Fallows "Success Without Victory," *The Atlantic*, January/February 2005.

Rami Khouri "Getting It Right in Iraq," *Maclean's*, May 19, 2003.

Douglas Little "David or Goliath? The Israel Lobby and Its Critics," *Political Science Quarterly*, Spring 2008.

Anna Mulrine "Overshadowed but, Sadly, Very Far from Over," *U.S. News and World Report*, July 31, 2006.

Steve Niva "Walling off Iraq: Israel's Imprint on U.S. Counterinsurgency Doctrine," *Middle East Policy*, Fall 2008.

Nir Rosen "Al Qaeda in Lebanon: The Iraq War Spreads," *Boston Review*, January/February 2008.

Patrick Seale "Gemayel, Syria, Israel and the War in Iraq," *Washington Report on Middle East Affairs*, January/February 2007.

The Iraq War and International Terrorism

The United Kingdom's Domestic Terrorist Threat Results from Factors Besides the War

Rod Liddle

In the following viewpoint the author, Rod Liddle, analyzes the wave of terrorist attacks in the United Kingdom since 2001. Liddle does not discount the influence of the Iraq War in radicalizing Muslim extremists, but describes other equally important motivations. He dismisses official pronouncements that terrorism is unrelated to Islam. Instead, he cites lax immigration and deep-set cultural differences as some of the reasons that Britain has seen an increase in terrorism. Rod Liddle is a journalist and former editor for the British Broadcasting Corporation (BBC).

As you read, consider the following questions:

1. According to the viewpoint, what groups have been assuring the British public that recent terrorist attacks are unrelated to Islam?

2. According to the poll referenced in the viewpoint, what percentage of British citizens believe there are too many immigrants in the country?

Rod Liddle, "The Public Know How These Attacks Happen—Unlike the Politicians," *Spectator*, July 7, 2007. www.spectator.co.uk. Reproduced by permission of *Spectator*.

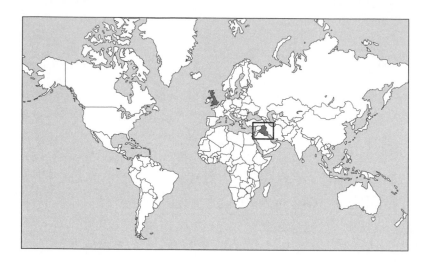

3. According to the author, does the majority of the British public support or oppose the war in Iraq?

'Al-Qa'eda brain surgeons fail to blow up large car full of petrol' has an agreeable ring to it, as a sort of taunt at our enemies and as a comfort blanket while we're standing in the mile-long queue at Heathrow with a sniffer-dog's snout in our groins. There is a certain truth to it too—and one not yet remarked upon, in public at least, perhaps for superstitious reasons: they're pretty useless, aren't they? And have been for some time, now. Useless either with cool, state-of-the-art plastic explosives on the Underground, cunning toothpaste tube bomblets at the airport or, the new cruder approach—cars full of petrol to which they apparently forget to apply a cigarette lighter. Almost nothing they do works, usually as a result of their own incompetence and stupidity. Imagine: you join al-Qa'eda, take your medical exams, get a job in a British provincial hospital and spend years patiently plotting, awaiting the right moment and painstakingly growing your beard. An enormous investment of time, money and effort. And then you fill the car full of gasoline and propane and succeed only in setting yourself alight and incurring a few parking fines. Suicide bombers are, by definition, an evolutionary anomaly, a strictly counter-Darwinian development. Maybe the good gene pool has already been blown to smithereens and only the thickoes remain. We may have been left with the jihadist equivalent of Norman Wisdom, squeaking 'Allah u-Akhbar, Mr Grimshaw!' shortly before being arrested near Sandbach.

Conflicting Beliefs About Why Terrorism Occurs

Which I suppose is just as well, given our palpable confusion and double standards when faced with Islamist attacks on our soil. The perpetrators may not have been British born and bred (can anyone explain why this was seen as 'good news'?) and the car bomb itself a new, imported strategy—but everything else about the events of last weekend [July 2007] was same ol', same ol'—including the substance of the Prime Minister's response, even though he's a brand new Prime Minister.

More than half of [British] Muslims feel sympathy for suicide bombers in Israel.

We began with the usual and—this time—quite surreal assurances from politicians, Muslim leaders and, in particular the BBC [British Broadcasting Corporation], that the latest attacks were 'nothing to do with Islam'. This is what we always hear when a bomb has gone off, or failed to go off—and it was always a silly statement, based upon nothing more real than wishful thinking and a quick, thoughtless, unnecessary genuflection towards crowd control. On this occasion, though, it was subtly undermined by one of the perpetrators, doused in flames outside Glasgow airport, screaming 'Allah! Allah! Allah! Allah!' before being peremptorily battered by a passer-by. Also, they parked their car at a mosque—and yet, according to every bigwig, policeman and community leader interviewed, this was a mere case of coincidence. . . .

Then, as always happens, we had the next stage of wishful thinking. Led by the BBC's bizarrely pro-Islamist Frank Gardner, we were assured by assorted correspondents and politicians that Britain's Muslim community were, in their entirety, appalled and outraged by the attacks. Well, maybe they were—but how do you know? Did you ask 'em, Frank? Don't forget that more than half of our Muslims feel sympathy for suicide bombers in Israel and a fairly hefty minority (one in eight, at the last count) for similar action against the cockroach imperialist infidel scum (i.e. you and me) over here. Not to mention almost half of Britain's Muslims who want Sharia [Islamic] law in this country and do not remotely, therefore, share our norms and values.

We are told these sorts of things in order to stop us coming to unpalatable conclusions, because the government still clings, ever more precariously, to the vestigial tail of that discredited ideology, multiculturalism. Take, for example, the issue of immigration. The aspirant, useless bombers who missed their targets at Glasgow and London came here from Iraq, Jordan, Saudi Arabia, Pakistan. A recent Mori opinion poll commissioned by the government's Commission on Integration and Cohesion showed that almost 70 per cent of British people thought that we had let far too many immigrants into the country. This figure, incidentally, included almost half of all black and Asian British citizens polled. It was a remarkable poll not so much for its statistics, however, as for the strange response to those statistics. The establishment—the government, the BBC, the race charities and so on—professed themselves very worried and wondered what on earth should be done. A task force charged with dampening down trouble in the immigration hotspots, maybe? A few more lessons in English for the incomers and maybe fewer translators? But at no point did any of the powers that be suggest the one thing which an overwhelming majority of those polled wished for: an end to immigration. A moratorium. Or, at the least, an influx which was vastly reduced and better regulated.

Last year [2007] the director of enforcement and removals at Immigration and Nationality admitted that he hadn't 'the faintest idea' how many illegal asylum seekers there were running around the country.

Immigration and Terrorism

This suggestion, implicitly supported by almost 70 per cent of those questioned and opposed by only 10 per cent, was not even considered; it simply didn't figure on the radar. And you begin to understand why this might be when you remember that in 2003 the then Home Secretary David Blunkett insisted that he saw nothing at all wrong with unlimited immigration. And last year [2007] the director of enforcement and removals at Immigration and Nationality admitted that he hadn't 'the faintest idea' how many illegal asylum seekers there were running around the country, getting up to mischief or otherwise. The government doesn't think that immigration matters; the public does. And the public's disaffection for mass immigration is not a reflexive racism and insularity, as the government and the BBC would seem to believe, but a worry based squarely upon the observable effects.

Would al-Qa'eda have found it so simple to place a dozen foot-soldiers in the NHS if we had been a little more rigorous about who we allowed into this country and we were a little more choosy about where they came from? Isn't the public, on this issue, right—and proven to be right?

But then, even if we had been told that the 12 or so aspirant bombers were members of al-Qa'eda and about to launch an attack against British citizens, it is unlikely we could have done very much about it, even if we had their home addresses

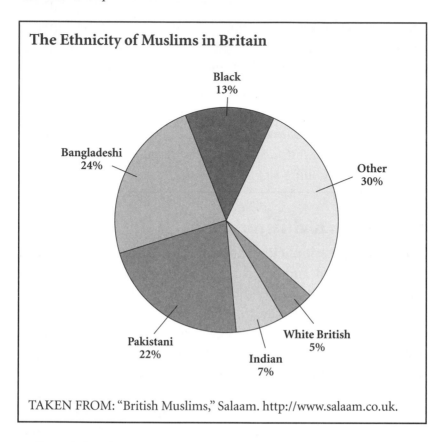

The Ethnicity of Muslims in Britain

Black
13%

Bangladeshi
24%

Other
30%

Pakistani
22%

Indian
7%

White British
5%

TAKEN FROM: "British Muslims," Salaam. http://www.salaam.co.uk.

and mobile phone numbers. Every month or so we read that the immigration appeals court has allowed some murderous lunatic from the Maghreb or beyond to stay in the country, despite his clearly stated homicidal impulses, because it would be an infringement of his human rights were he to be returned to the Islamic hellhole from which he arrived. Recently, for example, we had the case of 'A.S.', a Libyan extremist who was almost certainly a member of al-Qa'eda and with proven connections to the Muslim terrorists who had unleashed carnage in Madrid [Spain] and had planned to do so in Milan [Italy]. The appeals court accepted beyond all doubt that A.S. would most likely attempt to kill us all at some point in the future, because, frankly, that's the sort of chap he was. But it rejected the idea that he should be deported—or even locked up—because his safety, back in Libya, could not be absolutely guaranteed (and aside from coming here illegally he had committed no crime yet on British soil). Remarkably, the court conceded that it was highly unlikely that he would be in any real danger back in Libya but, Libya being a disagreeable sort of place, one couldn't be entirely sure. He was referred to as A.S., incidentally, so as to further protect his human rights.

The public is perpetually outraged by such clear absurdities and, on this occasion at least, the government seemed a little vexed too. But there was no resolve to enact legislation (or repeal existing legislation) to prevent such outrages occurring again. Faced with the law—and in particular, international treaties to which we gladly affixed our names in simpler times—the government feels and perhaps is impotent. It is surely only a matter of time before someone who comes before the immigration appeals court is allowed to stay and later blows himself up in a public place. Perhaps it has happened already.

I suppose we'll just have to put our faith in al-Qa'eda's continuing incompetence.

The Impact of Iraq

The overwhelming majority of the public is also opposed to the continuing war in Iraq, of course (although it has reached this conclusion a little late in the day for my liking). Whatever your feelings about the war, it must, surely, provide a moral justification for those Islamists intent upon unleashing murder upon our soil and at the same time, inculcate a deep sense of confusion within our Muslim community. Seen objectively, the aggression instigated by our political leaders against Iraq is no less motivated by a utopian, millennialist vision of how-the-world-must-be than the violence perpetrated by those who wish us all to be better off under the benevolence of a world caliphate. Evangelical liberal fundamentalism has led to rather more deaths in the world just recently than its fundamentalist Islamist counterpart: you might conclude that they are two sides of the same coin. This may seem to be an argument for cultural relativism of the worst kind; after all, we cleave to the values of liberal democracy because we know them to be right and thus worth fighting for—and, of course, imposing, at the point of a gun and a bomb, upon other people who may not yet have seen the light. Well, perhaps. But in which case it is difficult on objective grounds to adopt outraged expressions when those other people attempt to impose their equally implacable vision of how-the-world-must-be on us, at the point of a gun. This seems to me an incontestable proposition and has been advanced recently by people as philosophically diffuse as General Sir Michael Rose and John Gray, among many others. Yet it is antithetical to the government's point of view. But imagine for a moment that you are a British Muslim, suspended in a sort of demilitarised no-man's-land between the secular state and the long-held tenets of your faith. What conclusion would you reach about the competing claims of the war against terror and the war against the infidel? Might you not be inclined to ascribe to them an equivalence?

The odd thing is that on all of these issues—immigration, human rights legislation, the notion that British Muslims do not share very many of our liberal values, the war against Iraq—the public seems to get it and our political leaders simply do not. There will be many more attempts at carnage on our streets before they do get it, I suspect. In the meantime, I suppose we'll just have to put our faith in al-Qa'eda's continuing incompetence.

Withdrawing U.S. Forces from Iraq Will Increase Islamic Extremism

Reuel Marc Gerecht

In the following viewpoint, Reuel Marc Gerecht argues that a U.S. withdrawal from Iraq would not decrease international terrorism. Gerecht asserts that the roots of radical Muslim terrorism go far beyond Iraq and that if the United States removes its forces, Iraq would likely destabilize further. This destabilization would cause an expansion of terrorism since Iraq would likely become a base for future terrorist activities. Gerecht is a fellow at the American Enterprise Institute and a contributing editor to The Weekly Standard.

As you read, consider the following questions:

1. According to the viewpoint, what historical factors contributed to Islamic fundamentalism, prior to the Iraq War?

2. In the viewpoint, what country has replaced Saudi Arabia and Egypt as the main "breeding ground" of radical Islamic terrorism?

3. How many foreign fighters went to aid Afghanistan during the Soviets occupation in the 1980s?

Reuel Marc Gerecht, "Running from Iraq; Don't Imagine It Will Reduce the Jihadist Threat," *The Weekly Standard*, vol. 12, no. 6, October 23, 2006. Copyright © 2006, News Corporation, Weekly Standard. All rights reserved. Reproduced by permission.

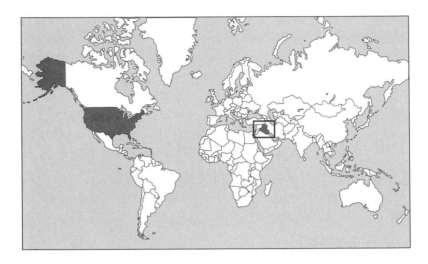

Is jihadism growing exponentially because of Iraq? The liberal parts of the press, Democratic politicians, and numerous counterterrorist experts say as much. They cite the classified National Intelligence Estimate (NIE) "Trends in Global Terrorism," completed in April 2006 but recently leaked in snippets, which they claim concluded that we are losing the fight against Islamic extremism because the war in Iraq is producing ever-expanding waves of holy warriors.

While it is surely true that jihadism is alive and well, and that the Iraq war has a role in its continued vibrancy, the insistence on a causal connection obscures a host of lasting factors that would powerfully fuel America-hatred whether or not the United States had gone back to Iraq. It also invites the fantasy that our exiting Iraq would leave us better off, when in all likelihood it would fan the flames of jihadism. . . .

The Impact of Iraq on Jihadism

Let us be absolutely clear: The war and its most tangible result—the empowerment of the Iraqi Shia and Kurds—have galvanized a Sunni jihadist cause in Mesopotamia. The Sunni will to power is a ferocious thing. Neither [*The Weekly Standard*] nor CIA [Central Intelligence Agency] and State Department analysts foresaw either the amplitude of this sentiment or the spread of fundamentalism among the Sunni community, widely deemed the bedrock of secularism inside Iraq. And the war has certainly provided riveting imagery and stories for Sunni holy warriors globally. It's reasonable to assume that the conflict has helped anti-American Sunni jihadists multiply their numbers.

Iraq, moreover, like Afghanistan during the Soviet-Afghan War, has provided a place where jihadists from different lands can meet, become blood brothers, and acquire deadly skills. Holy warriors in Iraq might learn something from Baathists turned Sunni supremacists. Saddam Hussein's Iraq trained many men to kill efficiently and savagely. When Saddam's Baathist totalitarianism spiritually ceased to exist, in its place, religious identities gained ground. Foreign holy warriors who hook up with ex-Baathists in Iraq will probably go home more dangerous than when they arrived—especially, as the NIE warned, if they go home victorious.

European and Pakistani holy warriors no doubt cite Iraq as one of America's sins, but beneath these declarations lie volcanoes rumbling from pressures much closer to home.

Al Qaeda spokesmen regularly declare that Iraq is at the center of their global effort to humble the United States, the great violator of Islamic lands and virtue. We should believe them—although their preferred battleground would still be America if they could figure out a way to put jihadist cells onto our soil. The [George W.] Bush administration and Muslim Americans, who have shown themselves highly resistant to the holy-warrior call, have so far kept al Qaeda from again fulfilling its dearest dream.

That's about all one can say for sure about the effects of Iraq on the global jihadist movement. Yet that's not where the

administration's critics like to stop. In their eyes, the Iraq war
has somehow ruptured the radical Muslim psyche in ways that
earlier events and preexisting factors did not.

Numerous Factors Spur Radical Muslims

In these critics' distorted perspective, the singular provocation
of the Iraq war trumps all the other well-known spurs to jihadist fury: the American flight from Beirut after the bombings
in 1983, the American flight from Somalia after "Black Hawk
Down," the attack on the U.S. embassies in Africa, the *USS
Cole*, 9/11 [2001 attacks on New York and Washington], the
continual bombing of Iraq under the Clinton administration,
the economic sanctions against Saddam's regime that Muslims
saw as choking the Iraqi people. The Iraq war, as the critics
see it, overwhelms the American attack on the Taliban and
[Osama] bin Laden, the Taliban's resurgence in Afghanistan,
bin Laden's survivor charisma, the Pakistani madrassa machine, General Pervez Musharraf's retreat from Waziristan, the
Saudi Wahhabi multitentacled missionary-money machine—
still the most influential conveyer of anti-American, anti-
Western, anti-Semitic, and anti-Christian hatred in the
world—the existence of Israel, the Israeli retreat from Lebanon in 2000, Palestinian suicide bombings, the resurgence of
Hezbollah, the triumph of American pop culture in Muslim
lands, the *Satanic Verses*, Danish cartoons lampooning the
Prophet Muhammad, the Western assault on traditional sexual
ethics and the God-ordained male domination of the Muslim
home, the constant, positivist legal assault on the Holy Law,
American and European support for Muslim dictatorships, the
Western-centered, Western-aping, increasingly brutal Muslim
regimes that have transgressed against God ever since Napo-
leon routed the mameluks outside Alexandria in 1798, and the
unbearable Western military supremacy that reversed a mil-
lennium of nearly uninterrupted Muslim triumphs. To these
critics, the Iraq war somehow is uglier than the whole cosmo-

logical affront of the modern world: Western Christians, Jews, and atheists on top; Asian Buddhists, Confucians, and Shintoists gaining power; the Hindu pantheists rising; and the Muslims, Allah's chosen people, descending.

All of this is downgraded before Iraq. It is particularly astonishing to see Iraq-centered critics discount the role of Pakistan and "post-Taliban" Afghanistan in fueling jihadism. It is arguable that Pakistan—not mentioned in the NIE's "Key Judgments"—has now replaced Saudi Arabia and Egypt as the intellectual breeding ground of jihadism. And what has been going on in Pakistan for decades has almost nothing to do with Iraq. European and Pakistani holy warriors no doubt cite Iraq as one of America's sins, but beneath these declarations lie volcanoes rumbling from pressures much closer to home. . . .

Islamic militants loathe Israel, which they view as a Jewish-Western colonial state occupying land vouchsafed to Muslims by God.

Sources of Radical Muslim Anger

Under Bush, these critics say, American foreign policy has become harsh and insensitive to Muslim feelings. Abu Ghraib, Guantanamo, secret CIA prisons, and other nefarious acts have supposedly given the United States a bad name among Muslims—as if we hadn't already squandered our credibility by failing to be a "fair and honest broker" in the Israeli-Palestinian conflict. These events have supposedly tarnished democracy and strengthened dictatorship in the region. Yet the most powerful force in Egypt trying to force democratic practices upon the dictatorship of Hosni Mubarak is the Muslim Brotherhood, and there is no evidence the Brotherhood wants democracy less because of American action in Iraq. Iraq may be going to hell in a hand basket, but it is an enormously dubious proposition that the powerless of the Middle East think better of their dictators because of the turmoil there. . . .

Islamic militants loathe Israel, which they view as a Jewish-Western colonial state occupying land vouchsafed to Muslims by God. There are very few mundane things that anger militant Muslims more than the "peace process," the attempt by the Americans and the Europeans to once again seduce Muslim rulers into actions betraying God, his Holy Law, and his people. But would administration critics want to walk away from the peace process because such negotiations infuriate radical Muslims, making their transformation into lethal anti-American holy warriors more likely?

Ditto for advocating women's rights among Muslims. The historian Bernard Lewis is right: The West's gradual liberation of women in their domestic and social roles is one of the principal factors behind the West's modern preeminence. And it has made the Islamic world's entry into modernity emotionally agonizing. The Franco-Iranian scholar Farhad Khosrokhavar (who recently published a fascinating study of members of al Qaeda in French prisons) summed it up nicely when he wrote:

> In removing the veil from Muslim women and in extolling a legal equality [between the sexes], which contravenes the laws of God and destroys the integrity of the family and its equitable sharing of duties between men and women, the West attempts to pervert the female race. According to the Holy Law, which [Muslim militants] interpret literally, refusing any evolution as a degradation of the faith's sovereignty, women ought to dedicate themselves to the family and the home while men remain masters of all that transpires in the public realm. The West smashes this fundamental relationship, sanctioned by God, through inseminating the virus of egalitarianism, hedonism, and sexual perversion. The liberation of women is thus in the same domain [for Islamic militants] as homosexuality and HIV. . . .

Anti-American Sentiment Is Unavoidable

The truth is that much of what the United States needs to do to win the war on Islamic extremism will naturally infuriate those who view the United States and American culture as threatening to Islam, all the more because they also find it appealing. Your average Muslim fundamentalist, who has no intention of becoming a holy warrior, fears and hates, and admires and envies, America. Such men and women are probably near a majority of all Muslims in every Arab land. Almost everything the United States does in this world ought to annoy these people. Much of what the United States needs to do will outrage them.

For example, the United Sates will continue to work with the security and intelligence services of many Middle Eastern autocracies. Unfortunately, the CIA is incapable of truly judging the value of such dealings since its bureaucratic interests are best served by inflating these "secret" relationships. But even if Egypt, Saudi Arabia, Jordan, and Pakistan contribute little to our well-being, in an age of mass-casualty terrorism, a bit of information at the right moment could matter enormously. We will deal with these distasteful regimes, and their subjects will understandably despise us for it.

Anti-Americanism is going to remain high.

Even if we ramp up our criticism of these regimes—and we should—and start to distance ourselves from them and condition our aid, we will still be condemned by many in the region for advocating democracy but supporting dictatorship. Nor are we going to stop supporting Israel or opposing terrorist organizations that are also popular social movements (Hamas and Hezbollah), or speaking in favor of women's equality and artistic freedom, or supporting our European allies who may (unwisely) decide to ban headscarves and other

Foreign Fighters Killed in Iraq by Country, 2003–2005

Main Countries of Origin	Percentage of 300 Confirmed Foreign Fighters* *7.7% was split among 11 other countries.
Saudi Arabia	55%
Syria	12.7%
Kuwait	5.3%
Jordan	4.7%
Libya	3.7%
Yemen	2.3%
Palestinian Territories	2.3%
Lebanon	2.3%
Algeria	2.3%
Tunisia	1.7%

Evan Kohlmann, "Foreign Fighters Reported Killed in Iraq: June 2003–June 2005," 2005. www.globalterroralert.com.

traditional Muslim practices within their countries. For these reasons and more, anti-Americanism is going to remain high.

What's more, if the Middle East evolves democratically— and the democratic conversation, amplified by the deposing of Saddam Hussein, remains vibrant—anti-Americanism will shoot through the roof. Fundamentalists will enter the public conversation even more loudly than they have already. Unless one believes that the regimes in place can kill off Islamic militancy and squash Islamic organizations that have terrorist movements within them, then the only solution to bin Ladenism is for Sunni fundamentalism itself to kill it off. Throughout much of the Islamic world, fundamentalism is now mainstream thought. But holding power will deprive militants of the luxury of mere opposition. In power and out, fundamentalists and more moderate Muslims will focus more seriously on Islamic political thought and practice. Under representative government, Muslims will have a harder time avoiding the rot—the ethics that allow young men to kill so easily. . . .

U.S. Support for Democracy in the Middle East

When Islamic activists become more responsible for governance, the fundamentalist civil wars will begin. (This process is starting in the Palestinian lands.) The introspection, debates, and fall from grace will be painful and quite possibly violent, as devout Muslims who incorporate the community's popular will into God's law fight it out with fundamentalists who view man-made legislation as an insult to Allah.

This contest is not what the Bush administration foresaw when it espoused democracy in the Middle East as part of the solution to the evil that struck us on 9/11 [2001]. But the president's democratic reflex was correct. And as faithful Muslims decide how much of Western political thought to incorporate into their own, anti-Americanism will skyrocket. Indeed, rising anti-Americanism will be a pretty good barometer of how serious the democratic-religious debates are in the Muslim Middle East. The more serious the debates, the more furious the flailing out against America by the hard-core militant Muslims will be.

The complexity of this picture suggests, among other things, how shallow the discussion has been among those who see our mistakes in Iraq as the epicenter of our terrorist problem. Discussion of what will happen if the United States pulls out of Iraq has been similarly thin.

Osama bin Laden has always claimed that he and his followers are the "strong horse" and that the United States is a "weak horse," unable to sustain a long war against the faithful.

A major American humiliation in Iraq would probably produce what the jihad-rising crowd think Iraq is already: an extraordinary stimulus to holy-warrior passion—Beirut, Mogadishu, the embassy bombings, the [*USS*] *Cole*, and 9/11 all rolled into one. The critics should at least try to make the argument that the hell we have now is worse than the whirlwind we will reap after we run.

A Collision Between Shiites and Sunnis

Of course, we might be lucky. The Iraqi Shiites could conceivably save us from seeing the jihadists triumph in Iraq. The Iraqi Sunnis won't. Their traditional social structure was mortally wounded by Saddam. The Sunni elite of Samarra, for example—probably the most bourgeois town in Sunni Iraqi—tried but failed to hold out against the radical Sunni supremacists, fundamentalists, and jihadists. The Sunni elders of Samarra actually cherished the Shiite Golden Shrine. They were its historic custodians, and often met within its confines, to talk politics and drink tea, before the men of violence blew it up. The odds are very poor that traditional Sunni hierarchies and the nonradicalized tribes outside of the major urban areas can withstand the Sunni radicals.

The Iraqi Sunni community has no grand ayatollahs and clerical structure of the Shiite kind to moderate and block its violent young men. Assuming the Shiites don't conquer the Sunni triangle, the Sunni community by itself will not spare us the sight of triumphant jihadists taking over American bases and planting their flags for all to see, courtesy of Al Jazeera's [Arabic-language news agency] satellite coverage. Try to recall an image of the mujahedeen winning in Afghanistan in 1989. You can't—there were few photographs of that distant war. But every man, woman, and child in the Muslim world will be flooded with vivid, lasting images of America's flight from Iraq.

Yet if the Shiites save us from the last-GI-out-of-Baghdad jihad recruitment videos by subduing the Sunni insurgency while we're still in Iraq, it will doubtless be by slaughtering all the bomb-happy Sunnis they can get their hands on. And that Shiite-Sunni collision could powerfully stoke the anti-American flames. The Salafis and Wahhabi fundamentalists loathe the Shiites, whom they view as mushrikun, those who ascribe partners to God. The Shiite charismatic view of history, where the Caliph Ali and his descendants, the imams, are indispensable intermediaries between God and man, is anathema to most Sunnis. In the eyes of many Sunnis in Iraq and elsewhere, the Iraqi Shia already carry the burden of being liberated by the Americans. If the Shiites are forced to conquer the Sunni triangle, which they probably will be, Sunni Arabs will blame the United States, perhaps with a new level of ferocity.

And neighbors will not stand idly by. The Saudi fundamentalists, apparently the largest contingent of foreign holy warriors in Iraq, would add one more item to their list of satanic things the United States has done. An overt and proud Shiite conquest of Iraq—which is probably inevitable if the Americans leave—would spook the Saudis, who would probably aggressively back their Wahhabi establishment's holy war against the Shia, supplying money and weapons to Iraq's Sunni Arabs.

The Jordanian and Egyptian Sunni establishments might do this, too, given their fear of a "pro-Iranian" Shiite bloc developing. In addition, the Jordanians would fear a tsunami of Sunni refugees from Iraq, threatening to change the politics and culture of Hashemite Jordan (think radicalization beyond the wildest hopes of Yasser Arafat). Foreign aid would prolong the conflagration in Iraq. It is worth recalling the explosion of Islamic radicalism that followed the Iranian revolution in 1979: The Saudis and Iranians went head to head in supporting their preferred Muslim radicals, a competition the Saudis decisively won, with Osama bin Laden a major beneficiary. A new battle between Sunnis and Shiites would spur missionary activity, perhaps on a scale not seen since the 1980s.

On the other hand, some helpful countervailing forces to the Sunni-Shiite explosion might come into play after an American retreat. What is striking about the conflict in Iraq is actually how few foreign fundamentalists have joined the fight. Iraq ought to be flooded with tens of thousands of die-hard militants, wreaking vastly greater havoc over much larger regions. Yet Arab and Pentagon reports from Iraq suggest that only a few thousand foreign jihadists have entered. Islamic fundamentalism is much stronger today than when the Soviets invaded Afghanistan in 1979. Yet the jihadist commitment to Afghanistan was greater than that seen today in Mesopotamia, the second most sacred land for historically sensitive Muslims.

Foreign Fighters in Afghanistan and Iraq

Figures for the Soviet-Afghan war are unreliable—they all come from Pakistani military intelligence. But the rough estimates were that 25,000 to 75,000 holy warriors came to Pakistan from 1980 to 1989. As crude as these numbers are, they still tell us something about the magnetism of Iraq and today's fundamentalist commitment to holy war. Also, we do not find the Egyptian Muslim Brotherhood, progenitor of modern Sunni fundamentalism, and its offshoots throwing their weight into this war. Why?

As the Israeli scholar Reuven Paz has noted, Egypt's dictator, Hosni Mubarak, may not want militants going to Iraq, as he once allowed them to go to Afghanistan, Bosnia, and Chechnya. And Egypt's Islamic activists themselves perhaps have looked into the moral abyss of holy war more acutely than most others because they witnessed the barbarism of some of their own militants in the past. They know Ayman al-Zawahiri firsthand. Egypt's Brotherhood, like its offshoots, has been a bit reluctant to embrace the global jihad of the truly hard-core. More deeply embedded nationalist sentiments may be the cause. In any case, something is going on here, something perhaps about the Sunni-versus-Shiite and Sunni-versus-Sunni strife, that makes one suspect al Qaeda's hopes for a triumphant Iraq campaign may not be requited—not if holy war brings as much discomfort as it brings glory. This could change if the Americans left and a vicious Shiite conquest of Iraq began. . . .

If the Americans flee, and the Shiites began a vengeful conquest of the country, Tehran, which is already making a play to lead the radical Muslim world, will reach out globally to Sunni holy warriors to divert attention from the Iraqi Shiite counterattack against Iraqi Sunnis.

One thing is highly probable: If the Americans flee, and the Shiites begin a vengeful conquest of the country, Tehran, which is already making a play to lead the radical Muslim world, will reach out globally to Sunni holy warriors to divert attention from the Iraqi Shiite counterattack against Iraqi Sunnis. The Iranian appeal will be to target America. All the expert discussion about Islamic terrorism now being the domain of "nonstate" actors will die a quick death at our expense. And the heretical Shiite Alawite regime in Damascus would likely echo this call, especially since the Syrian Sunni majority is becoming more devout. This would be an unintended, unpleasant consequence of the war in Iraq—of our mishandled counterinsurgency against the Sunnis and inadequate defense of the vanishing moderate Shiite center against ever-more powerful Shiite radicals. Neither the authors of the NIE on jihad nor the Democratic critics of the war apparently foresee this menace. . . .

Withdrawing U.S. Forces Will Only Make Things Worse

Once upon a time, the Iraqi army had a strong identity, which it often forced upon the rest of the nation, but that identity was inextricably connected to the Sunni governing class. Although there are many Sunnis serving in the new Iraqi army, their service to the country probably won't withstand the tough counterinsurgency that will be required to calm the Sunni triangle. Sunni participation in the government of Prime Minister Nouri al-Maliki, a Shiite, also will probably end with a serious counterinsurgency effort. Just remember how the Sunni elite acted when American forces reduced Falluja: Many went into open rebellion. Imagine how they would act if somebody tried to take down the city of Ramadi, the heart of Sunni rejectionism and power.

And it is equally unlikely that a Shiite-dominated army will be able to restrain its own kith and kin in the Shiite militias, at least while the Sunni insurgency thrives. They certainly won't be able to do so if they know the Americans are leaving. An American departure, be it rapid or gradual, anytime in the next few years would further stampede Iraqis to retreat to the security of their ethnic and religious communities. And U.S. threats to withdraw unless the Iraqis do a better job of forming a national-unity government and constraining their violent passions solicits from the Iraqis just the opposite of what is intended.

There are other reasons the American plans for a "political solution" to the insurgency and sectarian strife have been unsuccessful, but the Sunni, Shiite, and Kurdish divisions alone are sufficient to render null the "Iraqification" dreams of Republicans, Democrats, and General Abizaid. A forceful U.S. presence in Iraq was always the key to ensuring that Iraq's national identity had a chance to congeal peacefully—that the Sunni will to power was contained, that Shiite fear and loathing of the Baathists and Sunni fundamentalists didn't ignite into all-consuming revenge, destroying the Shiite center led by Grand Ayatollah Ali Sistani, and that Kurdish separatism didn't flare. We're beyond that now. But we're not beyond checking the worst tendencies within Iraqi society.

We are certainly not beyond the chance that the Iraqis can govern themselves more humanely than they were governed under Saddam Hussein. Whoever thinks Iraq is hell on earth now is suffering from a failure of imagination. If we leave, it will, in all probability, get vastly worse.

Indonesia and Other Countries Have Made Some Progress in Counterterrorism, in Spite of the Iraq War

Maria Moscaritolo

In the following viewpoint the author, Maria Moscaritolo, explains that counterterrorism efforts have had success in many areas of the world, with the notable exceptions of Afghanistan and Iraq. According to Moscaritolo, anti-terrorism efforts have been particularly effective in countries such as Indonesia, where many of the counterterrorism achievements have been the result of enhanced border security and efforts to curtail the financing of terrorist groups. Moscaritolo explains that national police forces have also increased regional and international cooperation, while some countries, including Australia and the United States, have bolstered aid for counterterrorism programs. Maria Moscaritolo is an Australian journalist and author.

As you read, consider the following questions:

1. According to the author, what country was the site of nearly half of all of the terrorist attacks in the world in 2005?

Maria Moscaritolo, "Glimmers of Hope: Can the World Claim Any Gains in the Trickiest Conflict?" *Mercury* (Hobart, Australia), May 4, 2007, p. 38. www.lexisnexis.com. © 2008 Davies Brothers Pty Limited. Reproduced by permission.

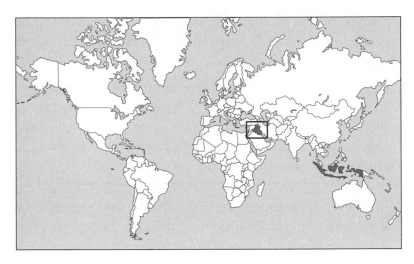

2. How much does Moscaritolo say Australia provided to neighboring countries to aid in the fight against terrorism?

3. According to the viewpoint, what countries are considered "state sponsors" of terrorism?

The one-step-forward, two-steps-backwards dance that is the "war on terror" appears to be making small progress.

Countries such as Indonesia are beginning to emerge from the mire, says the US [United States] State Department's latest Country Reports on Terrorism—but slowly, very slowly.

Terrorism in Iraq

Unsurprisingly, that's offset by deteriorating situations in such hot spots as Iraq.

If it wasn't for the doubling of terrorism incidents in Iraq and Afghanistan last year [2005], the world could perhaps be justified in giving itself a pat on the back for staving off a worsened circumstance in 2006.

The report, released only a few weeks after insurgents notched a significant victory by bombing the Iraqi Parliament in Baghdad's heavily fortified Green Zone, shows there were

6630 terror-related incidents in Iraq (in which 38,813 civilians were killed, injured or kidnapped, just under double the previous year) compared with 3,468 attacks in 2005.

Overall, the world has made progress in the unconventional global battle against terror groups, argues Frank Urbancic, the State Department's acting coordinator for counter-terrorism. . . .

In Afghanistan, there were 749 attacks last year affecting 2,943 victims, compared with 491 attacks in 2005.

So, Iraq accounted for almost half the 14,338 terror incidents worldwide last year.

Despite the obvious escalation in trouble, the report insists "international intervention in Iraq has brought measurable benefits", such as an emerging, although struggling, democracy.

Progress Against Terrorism

Overall, the world has made progress in the unconventional global battle against terror groups, argues Frank Urbancic, the State Department's acting coordinator for counter-terrorism; terrorists are being hampered by better border security, regional policing cooperation, a clamp-down on their finances, arrests and generally less freedom of movement.

"Working with allies and partners across the world through coordination and information sharing, we have created a less permissive operating environment for terrorists, keeping leaders on the move or hiding," says Urbancic.

"We've degraded their ability to plan and mount attacks. This has contributed to reduced terrorist operational capabilities, and detention or deaths of numerous key leaders."

The report noted Australia's strong counter-terrorism efforts in the region, with practical assistance and an extra $70 million to boost the capacity of neighbouring countries. Do-

The Indonesian Response to the 2002 Bali Bombings

The attack on Bali in 2002 began when a suicide bomber set off his explosive vest inside Paddy's Club at 11:08 p.m. The explosion is believed to have killed eight people, and it also drove panicked patrons out into the street, where another bomb was waiting. That bomb, a much bigger one hidden in a van ... was set off by a second man 29 seconds later, ripping through the crowds in the narrow street. . . .

The bombings ... galvanized the Indonesian government to act against Islamic militants after years of ignoring or failing to act on warnings from the United States and other nations that terrorists were active there. Since then, the government has made hundreds of arrests of suspected militants, including people accused of plotting attacks against United States interests overseas.

Raymond Bonner and Jane Perlez,
"Bali Bombings Kill at Least 25 in Tourist Spots,"
New York Times, *October 2, 2005.*

mestically, our efforts included arrests, new anti-money laundering and counter-terrorism financing legislation, and enhanced airport and border security.

The US report also applauded Indonesia's clamp-down on Jemmah Islamiyah and upgraded security at tourist sites but is critical of the slow pace of needed legal reforms.

"Indonesian counter-terrorism efforts remained hindered by weak laws and enforcement, serious internal coordination problems, and systemic corruption that further limited already strained government resources," it said.

Terrorists scored limited victories in our immediate region last year, with strikes mostly confined to the Philippines and Thailand, especially the problematic southern border.

Iran Is a Key Concern

Beyond Iraq and Afghanistan, Iran remains the key concern for America, followed by Sudan, Syria, North Korea and Cuba—countries the US refers to as "state sponsors" of terrorism.

"Iran continues to threaten its neighbours," says Urbancic. "It continues to destabilise Iraq by providing weapons, training, advice and funding to select Iraqi militants. As the President [George W. Bush] has said, some of the most powerful improvised explosive devices, IEDs, we are seeing now in Iraq include components that came from Iran."

It demonstrates that if Iraq was not a breeding place for terrorists at the outset in 2003, as some critics insist, it is now.

Terrorists Are Unconventional Enemies

Michael McKinley, senior lecturer in global politics and terrorism at the Australian National University, calls Iraq a "honeypot for terrorism".

"In some ways the symptom and its treatment are becoming integrated," says Dr McKinley.

"Iraq was never a centre for the promotion of terrorism, except against the Iraqi people themselves. Now it is. However, the longer you stay there, the more people [terrorists] you're going to get trained there. There's evidence that the techniques being used by the insurgents in Iraq are being transferred to Afghanistan—things such as the so-called IEDs, which were not so common in Afghanistan, are now apparently making their way there. The technology which is proving so effective in Baghdad is turning up in Kabul."

The report said although al-Qaida is still active and intent on further large-scale, anti-Western attacks, its top rungs have been disrupted, forcing it to intensify its propaganda campaign. It is maintaining presence and strength by "cynically exploiting the grievances of local groups and attempting to portray itself as the vanguard of a global movement".

"What they can't get by force they want to take by lies," is how Urbancic puts it.

Yet while this, and the relative stability of the past year, might imply terror outfits such as al-Qaida and JI are on the back foot, it would be foolish to assume any sort of victory.

As McKinley notes, terrorists are notoriously adaptable and any calm now may just mean a period of planning and regrouping:

"The problem with terrorism is that you never know when you might be attacked. It's not like a conventional enemy."

Indonesia had successfully broken up terrorist cells and made significant arrests.

Terrorism and Indonesia's Response

The report said Indonesia had successfully broken up terrorist cells and made significant arrests but also acknowledged police have to tread carefully not to further provoke militants by their operations.

So successes, in the short term, should be viewed cautiously, even pessimistically.

"It's possible in Indonesia that security agencies are having an effect," says McKinley, "but you'd want to see it [a drop in the number of attacks] over at least three years, and at best over five, because terrorist groups don't have infinite resources. They tend to act and then they need more resources."

Those resources include organisational leaders, some of whom have been killed or captured. Others, such as bomb-maker Noordin Mohammed Top, are on the run.

"Frankly, it hasn't got a great deal to do with security services," says McKinley. "It has more to do with resources available to a terrorist organisation."

American and British Intelligence Reports Indicate a Rise in Terrorism Due to the Iraq War

Neil Mackay

In the following viewpoint author Neil Mackay examines two intelligence reports, one British and one American, that were released in 2006. The reports indicate that the war in Iraq has fueled international terrorism. Countries such as Afghanistan and Pakistan have witnessed a dramatic rise in terrorism and, in the case of Pakistan, the Afghani leadership argues that the government has not done enough to suppress terrorism. Mackay asserts that the Iraq War has even led non-Muslim organizations to adopt some of the tactics of jihadist groups. Neil Mackay is an award-winning journalist for the Scottish newspaper the Sunday Herald.

As you read, consider the following questions:

1. What does the viewpoint describe as the main "recruiting sergeant" for radical Muslim extremists?

2. According to the viewpoint, what country's intelligence agency has allegedly been supporting Islamic terrorism in the form of military lessons?

3. How are terrorist groups using the Internet to expand
   their capabilities?

So, Britain and America's intelligence services believe that
the Iraq war has fuelled international terrorism aimed
against the West, and made the world a much more dangerous
place to live if you happen to come from Belfast or Boston,
Glasgow or Galveston, Manchester or Miami, Swansea or Se-
attle.

Leaked Intelligence Reports

Leaks, throughout the week [in September 2006], on the Iraq
war's "terror dividend" were deeply embarrassing to both
Whitehall and Washington. Evidence that both the invasion
and occupation of Iraq have, in the eyes of US [United States]
and UK [United Kingdom] intelligence, provided succour and
support for the international al-Qaeda franchise may have
come as something of a mild shock to ordinary British and
American citizens, but to intelligence operatives, military leaders and political insiders the revelation was a no-brainer.

Here is the bitterly sarcastic response from one British security source to news that leaked secret reports, from within

both the Ministry of Defence [MoD] and the American intelligence establishment, found that the invasion of Iraq was the number one recruiting sergeant for jihadi extremists: "No shit, really? What are you going to tell me next—that smoking gives you cancer?"

Not only have the leaked intelligence reports from Britain and America red-flagged just how counter-productive the war in Iraq has been, but they have also highlighted the fragmenting state of the alliances forged as part of the war on terror. As leaks dribbled out about what the spooks really thought about the fallout from the decision to hit Saddam, relations between the US and the UK, on one side, and Pakistan, on the other, turned increasingly sour.

British Assessments of the War on Terror

The head of Pakistan's Directorate for Inter-Services Intelligence (ISI) claimed, said President Pervez Musharraf, that former US deputy secretary of state Richard Armitage threatened to bomb the country into the "stone age" unless it supported the war on terror. This was followed by leaks from British intelligence that the UK's spying agencies felt the ISI had supported terrorism in Britain and Afghanistan. Amidst this East-West split, Pakistan and Afghanistan also fell out over who had or hadn't done the most to deal with Osama bin Laden's terrorist network and the Taliban.

The British leak came from the Defence Academy, a think-tank for the UK's Ministry of Defence. Written by a naval commander, it was a distillation of thinking from within the military and intelligence services. Its key finding reads: "The war in Iraq ... has acted as a recruiting sergeant for extremists across the Muslim world. . . . The al-Qaeda ideology has taken root within the Muslim world and Muslim populations within Western countries. Iraq has served to radicalise an already disillusioned youth and al-Qaeda has given them the will, intent, purpose and ideology to act."

It goes on to say that "the wars in Afghanistan and particularly Iraq have not gone well and are progressing slowly towards an as yet unspecified and uncertain result." So bad is the situation, that military brass want to pull out of Iraq so they can attempt to win the fight against the Taliban in Afghanistan.

The British government sent its troops into Afghanistan 'with its eyes closed.'

The paper says: "British armed forces are effectively held hostage in Iraq following the failure of the deal being attempted by the chief of staff to extricate UK armed forces from Iraq on the basis of doing Afghanistan, and are now fighting and are arguably losing, or potentially losing, on two fronts."

The West is "in a fix", the report says, adding that the British government sent its troops into Afghanistan "with its eyes closed". Senior British military commanders are now at loggerheads with their political masters over their desire to get British troops out of Iraq and into Afghanistan. For the time being, their efforts have been knocked down by the government. Troop levels will remain unchanged in Iraq for at least six months, although there have been hints that there might be a reduction in the British deployment to Iraq around the same time that Tony Blair leaves office.

Pakistan's Role

Next, the leaked British intelligence paper went on to attack Pakistan, saying:

"The army's dual role in combating terrorism and at the same time promoting the MMA [the hardline Mutahida Majlise-Amal, a coalition of religious parties], and so indirectly supporting the Taliban through the ISI, is coming under closer and closer international scrutiny. . . . Indirectly, Pakistan, through the ISI, has been supporting terrorism and extremism."

Some of the British suicide bombers who attacked the London transport system in July of last year [2005] had visited Pakistan. Other British-born Muslims have travelled to training camps in Pakistan.

There have been allegations that members of the Pakistani intelligence services provided military lessons at such camps.

Musharraf has hit back at such claims, saying that the London bombers were radicalised in Britain. "Let us not absolve the United Kingdom from their responsibilities," he said. "Youngsters who are 25, 30 years old, and who happen to come to Pakistan for a month or two, and you put the entire blame on these two months of visit to Pakistan and don't talk about the 27 years or whatever they are suffering in your country."

Musharraf tackled Tony Blair about the leaked report and its interpretation during a meeting on Thursday [October 2006]. The document also describes the British policy of supporting President Musharraf as flawed because Pakistan is "on the edge of chaos". It goes on to say that links between the British and Pakistan armies at a senior level should be exploited to persuade Musharraf to stand down, accept free elections and disband the ISI.

Government Reactions

MoD attempts to play down the leaked intelligence report were limp.

The Ministry said that the paper was just reporting the views of a variety of key personnel. However, as one senior military source said: "It is indeed the view of those in the military and in the intelligence and security services that Iraq was a mistake and that we need to concentrate on Afghanistan." The officer also said that it was "common knowledge—

The National Intelligence Estimate

We assess that the Iraq jihad is shaping a new generation of terrorist leaders and operatives; perceived jihadist success there would inspire more fighters to continue the struggle elsewhere.

The Iraq conflict has become the "cause celebre" for jihadists, breeding a deep resentment of US involvement in the Muslim world and cultivating supporters for the global jihadist movement. Should jihadists leaving Iraq perceive themselves, and be perceived, to have failed, we judge fewer fighters will be inspired to carry on the fight.

U.S. Director of National Intelligence,
"Declassified Key Judgments of the National Intelligence Estimate:
Trends in Global Terrorism: Implications for the United States,"
April 2006. www.oni.gov.

and had been for years" that the Pakistani intelligence service had aided the Taliban long before 9/11 [2001 attacks on the United States].

The MoD said that Pakistan was considered "a key ally in our efforts to combat international terrorism".

Officials added that Pakistan's security forces had made "considerable sacrifices in tackling al-Qaeda and the Taliban". Britain was also "working closely with Pakistan to tackle the root causes of terrorism".

America's 16 intelligence agencies were revealed to have concluded that the invasion of Iraq had also made the world a much more dangerous place to live.

Musharraf angrily attacked claims made about the ISI in the British intelligence paper. "I totally, 200%, reject it . . . ISI is a disciplined force, breaking the back of al-Qaeda. Getting 680 [al-Qaeda suspects in custody] would not have been possible if our ISI was not doing an excellent job."

Over on the other side of the Atlantic, the US administration experienced much the same kind of week as the British government when America's 16 intelligence agencies were revealed to have concluded that the invasion of Iraq had also made the world a much more dangerous place to live.

President Bush was eventually forced to declassify parts of his April 2006 National Intelligence Estimate (NIE) entitled *Trends In Global Terrorism: Implications For The United States*, following leaks in the US press.

One US intelligence analyst said of the document: "The leaks in the UK were embarrassing for the government, but they couldn't have been that much of a shock for many Brits. The leaks in the US, however, were really damaging. They came out just ahead of the midterm elections [for Congress in November]. . . . Our voters are still much more supportive of the war than those in the UK—so for them to hear from the intelligence services that the war increases the risk of terrorism is a major blow."

Jihadist groups will continue to hit 'soft targets', with fighters with experience of Iraq 'a potential source of leadership.'

The most damaging revelation in the NIE report was that "the Iraq conflict has become the 'cause celebre' for jihadists, breeding a deep resentment of US involvement in the Muslim world and cultivating supporters for the global jihad movement".

Al-Qaeda, according to US intelligence, is "exploiting the situation in Iraq to attract new recruits and donors and to maintain its leadership role".

The NIE also stated that the "global jihadist movement—which includes al-Qaeda, affiliated and independent terrorist groups, and emerging networks and cells—is spreading and adapting to counter-terrorism efforts", and that "activists identifying themselves as jihadists, although a small percentage of Muslims, are increasing in both number and geographic dispersion. . . . If this trend continues, threats to US interests at home and abroad will become more diverse, leading to increasing attacks worldwide. . . . The confluence of shared purpose and dispersed actors will make it harder to find and undermine jihadist groups."

The threat from "self-radicalised cells" will grow both "in the Homeland" and overseas. US intelligence notes that "jihadists regard Europe as an important venue for attacking Western interests. Extremist networks inside the extensive Muslim diasporas in Europe facilitate recruitment and staging for urban attacks, as illustrated by the 2004 Madrid [Spain] and 2005 London bombings."

Jihadist groups will continue to hit "soft targets", with fighters with experience of Iraq "a potential source of leadership".

Terrorism and Weapons of Mass Destruction

Disturbingly, the report adds that "CBRN [chemical, biological, radiological and nuclear] capabilities will continue to be sought by jihadist groups".

The NIE report also predicts that terror attacks against American and Western targets could spread out from Islamic groups to non-religious, non-Muslim organisations. "Anti-US and anti-globalisation sentiment is on the rise and fuelling other radical ideologies. This could prompt some leftist, nationalist or separatist groups to adopt terrorist methods to attack US interests. The radicalisation process is occurring more quickly, more widely and more anonymously in the Internet age, raising the likelihood of surprise attacks by unknown groups whose members and supporters may be difficult to pinpoint. We judge that groups of all stripes will increasingly use the Internet to communicate, propagandise, recruit, train, and obtain logistical and financial support."

The Political Reaction in the US

It's clear that the NIE assessment was leaked in the run-up to the Congressional elections in order to destabilise a Republican Party that bases its electoral appeal on tough security policies.

Senator Jay Rockefeller [D-WV], the lead Democrat on the intelligence committee, said: "There is no question that many of our policies have inflamed our enemies' hatred toward the United States and allowed violence to flourish. But it is the mistakes we made in Iraq—the lack of planning, the mismanagement and the complete incompetence of our leadership—that has done the most damage to our security." It wasn't just Democrats who turned on the administration. Republican senator Arlen Specter [R-PA] said he was "very concerned" about what the NIE assessment contained, adding: "My feeling is that the war in Iraq has intensified Islamic fundamentalism and radicalism."

The White House tried to spin the findings of the NIE paper, with Bush saying that it was only 'because of our success against the leadership of al-Qaeda [that] the enemy is becoming more diffuse and independent'.

Major General John Batiste, former commander of the 1st Infantry Division in Iraq in 2004–5 and also one-time military assistant to ex-deputy defence secretary Paul Wolfowitz, called for the resignation of defence secretary Donald Rumsfeld and said that the government "did not tell the American people the truth for fear of losing support for the war in Iraq".

The White House tried to spin the findings of the NIE paper, with Bush saying that it was only "because of our success against the leadership of al-Qaeda [that] the enemy is becoming more diffuse and independent". Intelligence sources on both sides of the Atlantic mocked the attempt to put a gloss on the facts as "pathetic".

Tony Snow, the White House press spokesman, also tried to accentuate the positive, saying: "Let's start with the obvious: since September 11, 2001, we have not been attacked. . . . We have kept America safe and we will continue to do so." His words came amid a military announcement that the number of suicide attacks in Iraq was at its highest-ever level since the invasion.

Homeland Security adviser Frances Fargos Townsend attacked the press for leaking the report, saying that they were endangering national security.

Bush also had to contend with trying to patch up the relationship between Pakistan and Afghanistan when the nations' two leaders—Pervez Musharraf and Hamid Karzai—were dinner guests of the president in Washington. The pair, who didn't even shake hands, have bitterly disagreed on how to fight the Taliban in the border areas between Pakistan and Afghanistan. Karzai says Pakistan is not doing enough to fight militants and deal with Taliban supporters operating in Pakistan and preparing attacks on Afghanistan. In reply, Musharraf has accused Karzai of doing little to deal with the Taliban and ignoring huge swathes of the country.

Bush also faces a revivified Bill Clinton wading into the November battle and playing the national security card. Clinton put the wind up the Republicans recently when he took an angry swipe at the Bush administration for its failures in tackling terrorism.

As one British intelligence analyst, who has worked closely with Washington, said: "There was only so long that the administrations in both London and Washington could go on pretending that everything was OK. . . . It's probably lucky for both Bush and Blair that the pair of them are coming to the end of their leaderships. I don't know how much more disastrous news the public can take about what they did in Iraq."

Periodical Bibliography

The following articles have been selected to supplement the diverse views presented in this chapter.

Nabeel Abraham	"From Baghdad to New York: Young Muslims on War and Terrorism," *Muslim World*, October 2005.
Daniel Benjamin	"Why Iraq Has Made Us Less Safe," *Time*, July 18, 2005.
Stephan Biddle, Michael O'Hanlon, and Kenneth Pollack	"How to Leave a Stable Iraq," *Foreign Affairs*, September/October 2008.
Christopher Dickey, John Barry, and Gameela Ismail	"Has the War Made US Safer?" *Newsweek*, April 14, 2004.
Caroline Elkins	"The Wrong Lesson," *The Atlantic*, July/August 2005.
David Enders	"Iraqis Seek to Stem Sectarian Violence," *The Nation*, December 8, 2006.
Esquire	"The End of the War on Terror," October 2008.
Foreign Policy	"The Terrorism Index," September/October 2007.
Richard Lowery	"What Went Right," *National Review*, May 9, 2005.
George Packer	"Knowing the Enemy," *The New Yorker*, December 18, 2006.
Jay Tolson	"The Coming Storms," *U.S. News and World Report*, March 14, 2005.
Hakan Tunc	"What Was It All About After All? The Causes of the Iraq War," *Contemporary Security Policy*, August 2005.

GLOBALVIEWPOINTS

CHAPTER 4

The Iraq War
and Democracy

The United Kingdom and Partners Have Helped Iraq Toward Democratic Self-Governance

Tony Blair

In the following viewpoint, former British Prime Minister Tony Blair provides an overview of the accomplishments of the international coalition that invaded and occupied Iraq. He details the challenges facing the new Iraqi government and discusses the strategies that the United Kingdom and the United States have devised, in consultation with the Iraqis, to overcome these hurdles. Blair also links the war in Iraq with broader anti-terror efforts around the world. Blair served as prime minister of the United Kingdom from 1997–2007 and was a staunch ally of U.S. President George W. Bush.

As you read, consider the following questions:

1. According to the viewpoint, what group is responsible for most of the suicide attacks in Iraq?

2. Where does the majority of violence occur in Iraq, according to the author?

3. According to Blair, what are the main tasks of the remaining British troops in Iraq?

Tony Blair, "Statement on Iraq and the Middle East," Speech to Parliament, February 21, 2007. www.number10.gov.uk. Reproduced by permission.

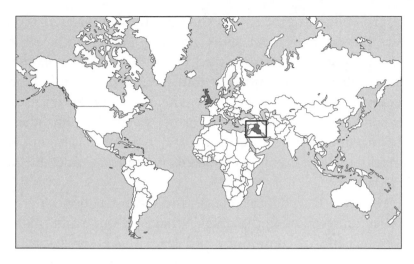

$\mathbf{S}$addam [Hussein, the ruler of Iraq] was removed from power in May 2003. In June of 2004 the UNSC [United Nations Security Council] passed a resolution setting out the support of the international community for the incoming Interim Government of Iraq, for a political process leading to full democratic elections overseen by the UN itself and for Iraq's reconstruction and development after decades of oppression and impoverishment under Saddam's dictatorship.

In January 2005 the first elections were held for a Transitional National Assembly. Seven million people voted. A new constitution was agreed. In December 2005 full Parliamentary elections were held. Twelve million Iraqis voted and in May 2006 the first fully elected Government of Iraq was formed. It was expressly non-sectarian, including all the main elements of Iraqi society—Shia, Sunni and Kurdish. Throughout there has been full UN backing for the political process and now for the Government of Prime Minister [Nouri al-] Maliki.

The Political Process

Successive UN Resolutions have given explicit approval for the presence of the MNF [Multi-National Force].

The political process has thus continued through these years. For example, as we speak, the Iraqi Parliament is awaiting the report on amending the Constitution from its Constitutional Review Committee; a draft law on de-Baathification, [removing members of the old regime, the Baath Party] relaxing some of the restrictions on former Baath Party members; and the new hydrocarbon legislation which will attempt to spread fairly and evenly the proceeds of Iraq's considerable oil wealth.

However, the political process, the reconstruction, the reconciliation, everything that the UN have set out as the will of the international community and Iraqis have voted for, has been thwarted or put at risk by the violence and terrorism that has beset the country and its people. From the appalling terrorist outrage in August 2003 that killed the UN Special Representative and many of his colleagues to this day, Iraq and Baghdad in particular has been subject to a sickening level of carnage, some aimed at the MNF but much aimed deliberately to provoke a sectarian struggle between Sunni and Shia. The bombing of the shrine at Samarra in February 2006 was designed precisely to provoke Shia death squads to retaliate against Sunni.

Talk to anyone in Iraq of whatever denomination, whether Iraqi, or part of the MNF, whether civilian or military, and they all say the same thing: the majority of Iraqis do not want it to be like this. They voted despite the violence. They know its purpose and its effect and they hate both.

The Insurgency

The violence comes from different sources. Some of it originates with former Saddamists; some with Sunnis who are worried that they will be excluded from the political future of Iraq. Much of the so-called "spectacular" suicide bombings are the work of al-Qaida whose grisly presence in Iraq since 2002 has been part of their wider battle with the forces of progress across the world. Now Shia militant groups like Jaish-al Mahdi—JAM—are responsible for the abduction and execution of innocent Sunni.

These groups have different aims, different ideologies, but one common purpose: to prevent Iraq's democracy from working.

Throughout all the wretched and inexcusable bloodshed, one hope remains. Talk to anyone in Iraq of whatever denomination, whether Iraqi, or part of the MNF, whether civilian or military, and they all say the same thing: the majority of Iraqis do not want it to be like this. They voted despite the violence. They know its purpose and its effect and they hate both.

There are now 10 divisions of the Iraqi Army, over 130,000 soldiers, able in significant parts of the country to provide order.

The Plan for the Future

There can be legitimate debate about what was right and what was wrong in respect of the original decision to remove Saddam. There can be no debate about the rights and wrongs of what is happening in Iraq today. The desire for democracy is good. The attempt to destroy it through terrorism is evil. Unfortunately that is not the question. The question is: not should we, but can we defeat this evil; do we have a plan to succeed?

Since the outset our plan, agreed by Iraq and the UN, has been to build up Iraqi capability in order to let them take control of their own destiny. As they would step up, we would, increasingly, step back. For three years therefore we have been working to create, train and equip Iraqi Security Forces ca-

161

pable of taking on the security of the country themselves. In normal circumstances, the progress would be considered remarkable. There are now 10 divisions of the Iraqi Army, over 130,000 soldiers, able in significant parts of the country to provide order. There are 135,000 in the Iraqi Police Service. There the progress has been more constrained and is frequently hampered by corruption and sectarianism but nonetheless, again, in normal circumstances it would be considered a remarkable effort. The plan of General [David] Petraeus—then an Army Commander in Iraq, now the Head of the Coalition forces there—which was conceived in 2004 has in its essential respects been put in place.

But these are not normal circumstances. The Iraqi Forces have often proved valiant. But the various forces against them have also re-doubled their efforts. In particular in and around Baghdad where 80–90 per cent of the violence is centred, they have engaged in a systematic attempt to bring the city to chaos. It is the capital of Iraq. Its strategic importance is fundamental. There has been an orgy of terrorism unleashed upon it in order to crush any possibility of it functioning.

There can be only one purpose in Iraq: to support the Government and people of the country to attain the necessary capability to run their own affairs as a sovereign, independent state.

Changes on the Ground

It doesn't much matter if elsewhere in Iraq—not least in Basra—change is happening. If Baghdad cannot be secured, the future of the country is in peril. The enemies of Iraq understand that. We understand it.

So, last year, in concert with our Allies and the Iraqi Government, a new plan was formulated, and promulgated by President Bush in January of this year [2007]. The purpose is

British Troops in Iraq

Year	Number of Troops
2003	40,000
2004	8,900
2005	8,500
2006	7,200
2007	5,500
2008	4,200
2009	2,500 (planned)

Figures are the yearly average and are rounded to the nearest 100.

Compiled by the editor.

unchanged. There can be only one purpose in Iraq: to support the Government and people of the country to attain the necessary capability to run their own affairs as a sovereign, independent state.

But the means of achieving the purpose were adjusted to meet the changing nature of the threat. . . .

There are three elements to the plan. First, there is the Baghdad Security Initiative, drawn up by Prime Minister Maliki and currently underway. It aims, like the Operation in Basra has done, to take the city, district by district, drive out the extremists, put the legitimate Iraqi Forces in charge and then make it fit for development, with a special fund in place able to deliver rapid improvement.

It began last Tuesday [February 13, 2007]. It is far too early to tell its results, though early indications are more promising than what was tried, unsuccessfully, some months back. In particular, there is no doubt of its welcome amongst ordinary people in Baghdad.

The second part of the plan is a massive effort to gear up the capability of the Iraqi Forces, to plug any gaps in command, logistics, training and equipment.

Thirdly, there is a new and far more focussed effort on reconciliation, reconstruction and development. There are now talks between Iraqi officials and both Sunni and Shia elements that have been engaged in fighting. It is again too early to draw conclusions, but this is being given a wholly different priority within the Iraqi Government and by the MNF.

In addition, there have been changes made by Prime Minister Maliki—to whose leadership I pay tribute—to the way economic development and reconstruction monies are administered within the Iraqi Government—with DPM [Deputy Prime Minister] Barham Saleh given specific responsibility. This will allow the disbursement of funds to be made and will allow, in Baghdad and elsewhere, development and reconstruction to follow closely on the heels of improved security.

Goals of the Coalition

The objective of all of this is to show the terrorists they cannot win; to show those that can be reconciled that they have a place in the new Iraq; and the Iraqi people that however long it takes, the legitimate Iraqi Government which they elected and which the international community supports, will prevail.

The aim of the additional US forces announced by President Bush is precisely to demonstrate that determination. If the Plan succeeds, then, of course, the requirement for the MNF reduces including in Baghdad. It is important to show the Iraqi people that we do not desire our Forces to remain any longer than they are needed; but whilst they are needed, we will be at their side.

In this context, what is happening in Basra is of huge importance. Over the past months, we have been conducting an operation in Basra, with the 10th Division of the Iraqi Army, to reach the stage where Basra can be secured by the Iraqis themselves.

The problems remain formidable, not least in providing work where for decades, 50 percent or more of [Basra] has been unemployed.

The Situation in Basra

The situation in Basra is very different from Baghdad. There is no Sunni insurgency. There is no al-Qaida base. There is little Shia on Sunni violence. The bulk of the attacks are on the MNF. It has never presented anything like the challenge of Baghdad. That said, British soldiers are under regular and often intense fire from extremist groups, notably elements of JAM. I would like, as I have often done in this House, to pay my profound respects to the British Armed Forces. Whatever views people have about Iraq, our Forces are dedicated, professional, committed and brave beyond belief. This country can be immensely proud of them. We send again our wholehearted sympathy to the families of those that have fallen, and the injured and their families also.

As a result of this operation, which is now complete, the Iraqi Forces now have the primary role for security in most parts of the city. It is still a difficult and sometimes dangerous place. But, many extremists have been arrested or left the city. The reported levels of murder and kidnapping are significantly down. Surveys of Basrawis, after the Operations had been conducted, show a much greater sense of security. There is reconstruction now happening in schools and health centres, around 300 projects altogether.

A few days ago, DPM Barham Saleh organised the Basra Development Forum. He announced a $200 million programme of development in infrastructure and public services. In addition, the international community—with Britain in the lead—has developed projects to increase power supply, put in place proper sewage systems, and increased the supply of drinking water to thousands of homes. The plan to develop Basra port will be published later this year. The problems remain formidable, not least in providing work where for decades, 50 percent or more of the city has been unemployed.

In an extraordinary development, the Marsh Arabs, driven from one of the world's foremost ecological sites by Saddam, have been able to re-settle there.

What all of this means is not that Basra is how we want it to be. But it does mean that the next chapter in Basra's history can be written by Iraqis.

UK-Iraq Cooperation

I have discussed this with Prime Minister Maliki and our proposals have his full support and indeed represent his wishes.

Already we have handed over prime responsibility for security to the Iraqi authorities in Al Muthanna and Dhi Qar. Now in Basra, over the coming months, we will transfer more of the responsibility directly to Iraqis. None of this will mean a diminution in our combat capability. The actual reduction in Forces will be from the present 7,100—itself down from over 9,000 two years ago and 40,000 at the time of the conflict—to roughly 5,500. However, with the exception of Forces which will remain at Basra Palace the British Forces will be located at Basra Air Base and be in a support role. They will transfer Shaibah Logistics Base, the Old State Building and the Shaat Al'Arab Hotel to full Iraqi control.

The British Forces that remain in Iraq will have the following tasks

- training and support to Iraqi Forces

- securing the Iraq/Iran border

- securing supply routes and, above all, the ability to conduct operations against extremist groups and be there in support of the Iraq Army when called upon.

Over time and depending naturally on progress and the capability of the ISF [International Security Force], we will be able to draw down further, possibly to below 5,000 once the Basra Palace site has been transferred to the Iraqis in late summer. We hope that Maysan Province can be transferred to full Iraqi control in the next few months and Basra in the second half of the year. The UK military presence will continue into 2008, for as long as we are wanted and have a job to do. Increasingly our role will be support and training, and our numbers will be able to reduce accordingly.

Throughout MND (South East) [Multi-National Division, a unit of foreign troops in Iraq] the UK depends on the steadfastness of our coalition partners—Denmark, Australia, Romania, the Czech Republic and Lithuania. I pay tribute to them. I welcome the continuing Australian role at Tallil in Dhi Qar province. We are keeping in close touch with our allies as the transition proceeds.

The speed at which this happens depends, of course, in part on what we do, what the Iraqi authorities themselves do; but also on the attitude of those we are, together, fighting. Their claim to be fighting for the liberation of their country is a palpable lie. They know perfectly well that if they stopped the terror, agreed to let the UN democratic process work and allowed the natural talent and wealth of the country to emerge, Iraq would prosper. We would be able to leave. It is precisely their intent to eliminate such a possibility.

Saddam inflicted one million casualties in the Iran-Iraq war and butchered hundreds of thousands of his citizens, including, by chemical weapons attack, wiping out whole villages of people.

Iraq and the Broader War on Terror

In truth, this is part of a wider struggle taking place across the region. The Middle East is facing an epochal struggle between the forces of progress and the forces of reaction.

The same elements of extremism trying to submerge Iraqi—or Afghanistan for that matter—are the same elements that across the region, stand in the way of a different and better future. None of this absolves us from responsibility. In fact, for too long, we believed that provided regimes were "on our side", what they did to their own people was their own business. We must never forget that Saddam inflicted one million casualties in the Iran-Iraq war and butchered hundreds of thousands of his citizens, including, by chemical weapons attack, wiping out whole villages of people.

We need now to recognise that the spread of greater freedom, democracy and justice to the region is the best guarantee of our future security as well as the region's prosperity. That is why peace between Israel and Palestine is not an issue inhabiting a different domain of policy. It is a crucial part of the whole piece. I shall meet President [Mahmoud] Abbas later today, talk to Prime Minister [Shud] Olmert, and within the last 24 hours have had detailed discussions both with President [George W.] Bush and Secretary [Condoleezza] Rice. I will once again emphasise the importance of basing the proposed NUG [National Unity Government, the government of Iraq] on the Principles of the Quartet. I will also stress our complete and total determination to use the new opportunity to create the chance for peace.

I have always been a supporter of the State of Israel. I will always remain so. But for the sake of Israel as well as for all we want to achieve in the Middle East, we need a proper, well functioning, independent and viable State of Palestine.

We should support all those across the region who are treading the path of progress—from the Government of Lebanon, whose Prime Minister courageously holds firm to democracy, to those countries, and there are many, who are taking the first fledgling steps to a different and more democratic governance.

Iran and Syria

As for Iran and Syria, they should not be treated as if the same. There is evidence recently that Syria has realised the threat al-Qaida poses and is acting against it. But its intentions towards Iraq remain ambiguous and towards Lebanon hostile.

The statements emanating from Iran are contradictory, but as the words yesterday [February 20, 2007] of the head of the IAEA [International Atomic Energy Agency] indicate, their nuclear weapons ambitions appear to continue. But both countries—though very different—have a clear choice: work with the international community or defy it. They can support peace in Palestine, democracy in Lebanon, the elected Government of Iraq—in which case they will find us willing to respond; or they can undermine every chance of progress, uniting with the worst and most violent elements, in which case they will become increasingly isolated, politically and economically.

Change Is Needed in the Middle East

But what nobody should doubt is that whatever the debates about tactics, the strategy is clear: to bring about enduring change in the Middle East as an indispensable part of our own enduring security. The poisonous ideology that erupted after 9/11 [2001 terrorist attacks on the United States] has its roots there, and is still nurtured and supported there. It has chosen Iraq as the battleground. Defeating it is essential. Essential for Iraq.

But also, now, for us here in our own country. Self-evidently the challenge is enormous. It is the purpose of our enemies to make it so. But our purpose in the face of their threat, should be to stand up to them, to make it clear that however arduous the challenge the values that they represent will not win and the values we represent, will.

The United Kingdom Has Failed in Efforts to Promote Stability and Democracy in Iraq

David Wearing

In the following viewpoint, David Wearing criticizes British participation in the Iraq War and British efforts to promote democracy and stability in the region. He argues that Britain was not prepared for the occupation of Iraq and that its political and military leaders made a number of mistakes after the invasion. In addition, the British have not been perceived as a legitimate governing force in Iraq and attacks on British forces have steadily increased. Wearing is a journalist and media commentator who specializes in British politics and the Middle East.

As you read, consider the following questions:

1. According to the viewpoint, what were Britain's two goals in the Iraq War?

2. According to Wearing, what percentage of the central government's revenue is provided by the four Iraqi provinces run by Britain?

3. How many attacks against British troops does the viewpoint claim occurred per day by early 2007?

David Wearing, "Britain's Failure in Iraq," *Le Monde Diplomatique*, November 2007. http://mondediplo.com. This article reprinted from *Le Monde Diplomatique*'s English language version, available online at www.mondediplo.com. Reproduced by permission.

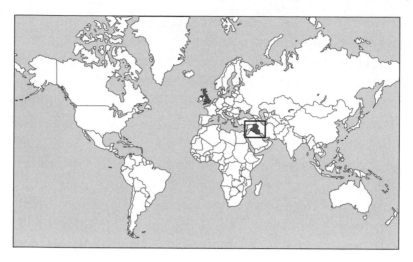

Last month's [October 2007] announcement of substantial withdrawals of British troops from southern Iraq is a useful vantage point from which to review Britain's part in the occupation. The role of the United States has been the more important, and is far better documented and understood. But Britain's role has not been insignificant, especially for the people of southern Iraq.

Britain's Goals

In 2003, Britain promised a post-Saddam [Hussein] Iraq that would be "a stable, united and law-abiding state providing effective representative government to its own people." That those ambitions have not been realised is now widely acknowledged even within the political establishment. A recent report by Michael Knights and Ed Williams described Iraq's deep south, the area for which Britain is responsible, as "a kleptocracy" where "well armed political-criminal mafiosi [organized crime members] have locked both the central government and the people out of power".

Britain's official goals have now been significantly downgraded to keeping violence at a manageable level, and leaving local administrators and security services to deal with the situation. Even this is far from being achieved, and Britain faces these problems in near isolation from the international community. British policy makers and analysts will be asking themselves what went wrong for many years to come.

While Washington's aim in Iraq was to establish a military presence and a client government in the heart of the world's principal energy producing region, securing a major source of global strategic leverage, Britain's aims were far less grand, as befits its status as a second-tier power. It sought to act as a transatlantic bridge between a sceptical Europe and the belligerent foreign policies of the US [United States] post-9/11 [2001 terrorist attacks on the United States], and to prove its worth as a military ally to Washington.

When its first major objective—acting as a transatlantic bridge—collapsed, Britain was left mostly isolated beside the US, and concentrated on its second aim: providing military support to the US-led occupation by running four provinces in the south.

Britain's Failures

But British diplomacy failed to dissuade Germany and France from objecting to the invasion of Iraq in 2003, and many of those European countries that did join the US-led coalition left as the post-war security situation deteriorated sharply. Even in financial donations to the Iraqi reconstruction effort, the European contribution was minimal, despite British pleas.

When its first major objective—acting as a transatlantic bridge—collapsed, Britain was left mostly isolated beside the US, and concentrated on its second aim: providing military support to the US-led occupation by running four provinces in the south. This area—containing 71% of Iraq's oil reserves and its second city and main port Basra (population 1.3 million)—provides 95% of central government revenue. The task was not insignificant, so it is all the more notable that the region has, according to Knights and Williams, "suffered one of the worst reversals of fortune of any area in Iraq since the fall of Saddam's regime".

Immediately after the invasion, Britain made two decisions that were crucial in precipitating the eventual collapse of order in the south. The first was the failure or refusal of British forces to prevent the looting that quickly followed the demise of the Ba'ath regime. Britain described this as a "redistribution of wealth" (an echo of Donald Rumsfeld's callous phrase "stuff happens"), demonstrating an unwillingness to discharge the responsibilities that it had unilaterally assumed by invading the south, and sending a clear message to various forces that an anarchic space would be available for them to exploit.

The second decision gave the lie to lofty Anglo-American rhetoric about spreading democracy throughout the Middle East. In May 2003 the US-led Coalition Provisional Authority (CPA) decided to clamp down on a spontaneous eruption of indigenous democracy already taking place at local level. Popular local councils had begun to form, with plans underway for small caucuses or even one man, one vote elections.

British rule did not prove effective either for Iraqi or British purposes.

Operation Phoenix

Seeing in this nascent self-government the threat of a new Iraq forming in an unsuitable manner, the British, on orders from CPA Baghdad, launched Operation Phoenix, described by Knights and Williams as "a civil-military operation to dissolve all unofficial councils and remove them from government premises". By occupation decree, municipal government was to be run by Iraqis hand-picked by the coalition, a measure which led thousands to take part in public demonstrations denouncing British rule as anti-democratic. One might speculate as to how local government would have fared in securing political stability if homegrown systems of administration had been allowed to develop naturally and by common consensus.

British rule did not prove effective either for Iraqi or British purposes. Unlike the brutal approach taken by the US in Baghdad and central Iraq, Britain preferred to choose those local actors most favourable, or least unfavourable, to its interests, and then to stand in the background as much as possible. By cultivating links with the coalition, the Iranian-backed Islamist group Sciri (now Siic) was able to take the role of local enforcer at an early stage. Local government positions fell easily into its grasp, while its Badr militia took over the security services and ran death squads to eliminate former Ba'athists and any potential moderate, secular opposition. Though it was clear that Badr was responsible for many atrocities, Britain was unwilling or unable to stop it.

Elections, held earlier than the CPA had planned following massive national demonstrations, brought other Islamist parties (principally Fadhila and the Sadrists) into the picture. The new order rejected the authority of central government and of the British, filling local security forces with party-militia personnel and turning local government into a spoils system to embezzle the region's wealth.

As the parties began to act like mafia gangs and turf wars broke out, Britain realised it had serious problems and attempted to break the power of the militias. But it was too late. The factions were prepared to defend the spoils system and refused to bow to a foreign authority that was widely viewed as illegitimate. Attacks on British troops rose from 1.2 a day between February and June 2005 to eight a day between February and May 2007.

In August 2006 the British were forced to abandon Camp Abu Naji near Amarah under heavy fire from the Sadrist Mahdi army. That October most of the staff of the British

British Government Investments in Iraq

- Between 2003 and 2007 DFID [the British Department for International Development] has invested around £78 million in essential infrastructure repairs in southern Iraq.
- The above projects were overseen by Iraqi contractors and have created approximately 25,000 work days for Iraqis.
- Since 2003, DFID has increased water supply by up to 30 percent in some provinces, and improved the electricity supply to 1.5 million residents in Basra. We have replaced 200 kilometres of water mains in southern Iraq.
- The UK [United Kingdom] has committed a total of £744 million towards Iraq, and has fully disbursed the £544 million pledged at the Madrid Donors' Conference in October 2003. Further pledges of £200 million have been announced by the Chancellor of the Exchequer and the Foreign Secretary.

United Kingdom Department for International Development,
"Better Basra: Getting Clean Water to Southern Iraq,"
June 20, 2007. www.dfid.gov.uk.

consulate in Basra had to relocate to the remote base near the local airport, under heavy mortar fire. Operation Sinbad, a last-ditch initiative similar to the US surge, provided only a brief and fleeting illusion of security. In September 2007 the British army withdrew from its last base in Basra city, repositioning its remaining troops at the airport. Now many of them are scheduled to be withdrawn early in 2008.

Britain's Future in Iraq

What are the prospects for Britain's future involvement in Iraq? The prime minister, Gordon Brown, has said any continuing military presence will be justified only on the basis of advice from his generals. Yet senior military commanders have already said that Britain can achieve nothing more in Iraq. In fact, it is as much the strategic Anglo-American relationship as the military realities on the ground that define the British mission, and cast doubt on the likelihood of a complete British withdrawal in the near future. For example, the withdrawal from Basra palace to the airport outside the city was, according to a senior British officer, delayed for five months due to political pressure from Washington.

The US clearly plans a long-term military presence in Iraq and is unlikely to want the British presence to be any shorter. The US needs protection for its supply lines from the Gulf and, for domestic political purposes, to sustain the illusion of being part of an international coalition. Downing Street may only be able to offer limited troop draw-downs to mollify voters and a restive military.

What caused Britain's failures in Iraq? Two key factors can be identified: a lack of capability and of legitimacy. Britain is experiencing a miniature version of the current US imperial overstretch. Britain had neither the diplomatic influence to act as an effective transatlantic bridge nor the military capacity to control its zone of operation in the south. It has found that attempts to conquer third world countries in the 21st century are not as feasible as they were in the 19th century. Decades of anti-colonial struggles, military and political, have engendered a substantial ability to resist domination.

Britain joined the invasion of Iraq with an inflated sense of its diplomatic and military capacity, coupled with a casual disregard for the wishes and rights of the Iraqi population.

Moreover, while Britain and the US have adopted different approaches to counter-insurgency in their respective areas, what they have had in common was always more important: a lack of legitimacy among the population (unlike the regional government of the Kurdish north). Britain has claimed legitimacy for its presence in Iraq on the basis of an endorsement by the UN [United Nations] Security Council. But a decision taken by 15 foreign governments in New York can hardly legitimise an occupation opposed by the majority of the Iraqi population. An occupation cannot be sustained in such circumstances.

Britain joined the invasion of Iraq with an inflated sense of its diplomatic and military capacity, coupled with a casual disregard for the wishes and rights of the Iraqi population that long predates even British government backing for Saddam Hussein in the 1980s. As a result, five years after the Blair government's propaganda drive about Iraq's alleged weapons of mass destruction, the presence of a dwindling number of British troops on the outskirts of Basra and the violent disintegration of Iraqi society in the south are now all that remain of Britain's policy.

The United States' Inability to Stabilize Iraq Has Undermined Efforts to Promote Democracy

Harold E. Rogers Jr.

In the following viewpoint, Harold E. Rogers Jr. examines the reasons why the United States has had such difficulties in containing the insurgency in Iraq. Rogers describes the reasons behind the U.S. effort to develop a democracy in Iraq and why those efforts have been stymied. He also links Iraq with past attempts by the United States to spread democracy in countries such as Vietnam. Rogers is a former military officer and the author of The History of Democracy from the Middle East to Western Civilizations.

As you read, consider the following questions:

1. According to Rogers, what is the main difference between Sunni and Shiite Muslims?

2. Who was the first woman elected Speaker of the House of Representatives in the United States?

3. What Middle East countries were created after World War I?

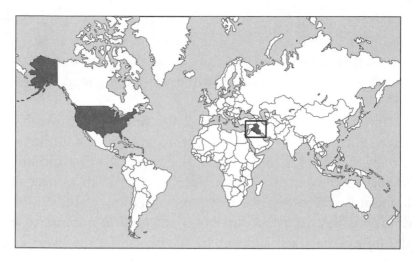

George W. Bush has been racing around the globe, as many presidents do during the last two years of their terms, trying his best to keep the ship of state afloat. However, almost every day, or at least every week, he seems to face a new crisis in Europe, Latin America, North Korea, Iraq, Iran, or Washington, D.C. The President certainly has grown in his job and is to be commended for his ability to jump from crisis to crisis, with an appropriate speech in hand, and to give the appearance of continued good health. Perhaps part of Bush's secret is being single-minded, some might even say stubborn, in defending what he believes is the basic winning theme of his presidency: keeping the U.S. safe from terrorists.

Iraq and the War on Terrorism

The President uses what he hopes is a conclusive argument when any citizen or, particularly, member of Congress, raises the question, "When are the troops coming home from Iraq?" Bush says that if we do not fight the terrorists in Iraq and instead pull out our troops in a cut-and-run fashion, the terrorists will follow us home and we will have to fight them on Main Street. Like most political arguments, this one partially is true, but hardly conclusive. Terrorists without doubt can penetrate our defenses and blow themselves up after they reach our homeland. While our defenders can stop most terrorists, they cannot stop them all, especially those who believe that they immediately will go to heaven if they martyr themselves.

In any war, it is hard to predict all outcomes. Our armed forces must do their best, however, to anticipate and prepare for any threats to the nation—and certainly, the first and most important duty of the commander in chief is to protect the homeland and to preserve our democratic way of life. Bush is doing his best to carry out this mandate, but appears to be sliding off the track laid out by his overseers, the American electorate. Bush has seen his approval rating plummet from extreme highs at the time U.S. troops captured Baghdad to unprecedented lows as the country finds itself bogged down in a civil war between the Sunnis and Shiites of Iraq. The principal difference between the two sects is that the Sunnis believe that the successor to Muhammad, who died in the year 632, should be elected (perhaps democratically), while the Shiites insist that the successor must be a direct descendent of Muhammad. There is no way the U.S. can win a civil war in Iraq. Saddam Hussein kept warring tribes under control by vicious tactics using his political parties (the Bathists) as spies and then rounding up the dissidents and shooting or gassing them.

With the weapons of mass destruction argument for the war disappearing, and the electorate becoming impatient, Bush tried to create a new justification: forging democracy in the Middle East.

The Iraq Insurgency and Democracy

Bush was convinced he could handle the problem a different way. His troops had failed to find weapons of mass destruction, his original justification for the U.S. invasion. In May

2003, in a grand gesture, the President flew to the *USS Lincoln*, an aircraft carrier steaming off the coast of San Diego and, with a huge banner in the background emblazoned with the words "Mission Accomplished," Bush declared that the heavy fighting was over. However, he did not count on the insurgents rearming themselves with the help of Syria, Iran, and others. The Iraqi war has claimed more than 3,500 lives, while over 24,000 others have been wounded. The war is in its fourth year, and the electorate has had enough. A majority believe it was a bad idea to initiate this conflict and that the U.S. should bring the troops home.

With the weapons of mass destruction argument for the war disappearing, and the electorate becoming impatient, Bush tried to create a new justification: forging democracy in the Middle East. In his second inaugural address, the President laid out his world vision for the next four years. War still was raging in Iraq and the first of a series of elections was scheduled there 10 days later. He spoke in sweeping terms: "The survival of liberty in our land increasingly depends on the success of liberty in other lands. The best hope for peace in our world is the expansion of freedom in all the world. . . . Every man and woman on this Earth has rights, and dignity and matchless value, because they bear the image of the Maker. . . . We have proclaimed the imperative of self-government because no one is fit to be a master and no one deserves to be a slave. Advancing these ideals . . . is the urgent requirement of our nation's security, and the calling of our time. . . . So, it is the policy of the United States to seek and support the growth of democratic movements and institutions in every nation and culture with the ultimate goal of ending tyranny in our world."

As expected, the U.S.'s drive to plant democracy firmly in the Middle East, beginning with the Iraqi elections, ran into fierce opposition from the terrorists. Abu Musab al-Zarqawi, the since-assassinated Jordanian-born al Qaeda chief in Iraq, declared war on democracy in an audio recording posted on the Internet Jan. 23, 2005. He stated: We have declared a fierce war on this evil principle of democracy and those who follow this wrong ideology. Al-Zarqawi railed against democracy for supplanting the rule of God with the rule of man and the majority, and that this was based on un-Islamic beliefs such as freedom of expression and separation of church and state. If al-Zarqawi's statement of Muslim belief is accurate, the U.S. is faced with a wide gulf of Muslim disbelief when it tries to sell democracy in the Middle East.

Bush has ignored these recommendations [from the Iraq Study Group that advises a dialog with Syria, Iran and their neighbors], making it clear that he will not talk with any rogue nations as long as they are engaging in what he deems to be unacceptable behavior.

Pres. Bush's heart is in the right place wanting to bring the blessings of liberty and democracy to the Middle East. However, the longer the war lasts, the worse it seems to get. Bush, though, is out there cheering the troops on, declaring that our only acceptable goal is complete victory, for if we settle for anything less, all respect for us as the principal superpower will be lost. However, not everybody believes the President about the necessity of achieving complete victory, so his poll numbers have dropped. Bush initially raised a very high bar to measure the success of our mission, but steadily has lowered the bar as the war drags on and on without much—or any—progress.

Bush also opted for a change of command in Iraq, substituting Gen. David Petraeus, an officer with uniformly high marks, for his previous commanders in the field. Gen. Petraeus has advised the President that there is a chance of success if he is allowed to command an additional 20,000 or so troops in a surge to bring order to the chaos of Baghdad.

Most Democrats and a majority of the House of Representatives and Senate, while hopeful of success, are against this new surge. Bush had been used to dealing with a rubber stamp Congress, but now is faced with a Democratic majority in the House of Representatives and Senate. He also faces Nancy Pelosi, the first woman ever named Speaker of the House.

The Impact of the Democratic Congress

Bush has not yet quite figured out how to deal with the new Speaker. After guiding the recent budget through Congress, Pelosi, against the wishes of the President, led a Congressional delegation to the Middle East, where she had personal meetings with Prime Minister Ehud Olmert of Israel, Pres. Bashar Assad of Syria, Prime Minister Fouad Siniora of Lebanon, Pres. Mahmoud Abbas of Palestine, and with the senior officers of Saudi Arabia. Since the Speaker is second in line [after the vice president] to the nation's highest office should anything happen to the president, her presence in the Middle East was taken seriously. Bush and others have attacked her mission as sending mixed signals. However, she seems not to be bothered by the criticism. She was accompanied by a bevy of Democratic House members, including Tom Lantos, head of the House Foreign Relations Committee. This mission probably was helpful by carrying out some of the recommendations of the Iraq Study Group report prepared by a committee headed by former Secretary of State James Baker recommending that Bush open a dialog with Syria, Iran, and their neighbors. Bush has ignored these recommendations, making it clear that he will not talk with any rogue nations as long as they are engaging in what he deems to be unacceptable behavior.

A number of questions were raised over the Pelosi mission to the Middle East. Foremost, does the Constitution approve or disapprove of such activities? Under the checks and balances system, we have divvied up governmental power three ways. Congress legislates and provides money for and declares wars. The president is the commander in chief and carries out the laws. The Supreme Court interprets the laws. While Congress has the duty to oversee activities of the president, it nowhere states whether Congress may or may not conduct foreign policy. However, it would seem logical that the policy must be unified so as not to confuse the U.S.'s friends or foes. Congress clearly has fact-finding responsibilities—so it can carry out its duties of oversight properly—including approving ambassadors and other officers responsible for foreign policy.

The President now is in somewhat of a quandary since his time for finding an acceptable solution to the Iraqi war is running out. He desperately wants Congress to give Gen. Petraeus—who was, after all, approved as commander by that body—a chance. For his part, Petraeus is cautious during interviews and says that we will not know if the surge is successful for months. Yet, what if it is not? Does Bush have a Plan B? Moreover, what if U.S. troops simply left Iraq? How quickly could or would they depart? Where would the withdrawn troops be deployed—perhaps Kuwait, or their home bases? What would the U.S. do if terrorists rushed in to fill the vacuum?

Iraq and Past U.S. Wars

For answers, perhaps we should look at some of the long-term results of other wars involving the U.S. Vietnam was this country's longest and least popular war. When American troops finally pulled out of Saigon, the North Vietnamese rushed in. Yet, South Vietnam eventually prospered. Maybe that is not such a bad idea in the Middle East, as somehow, our bitter enemies have a way of becoming our new friends. Several years ago, my wife and I took a trip to Vietnam and we were struck by the friendliness of the native people; we asked them why. They explained that they had been invaded

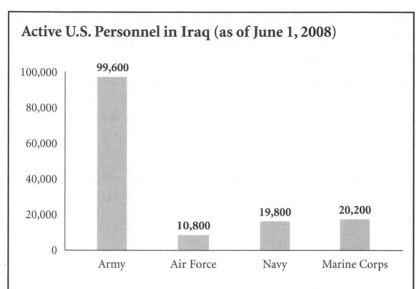

Active U.S. Personnel in Iraq (as of June 1, 2008)

TAKEN FROM: JoAnne O'Bryant and Michael Waterhouse, "U.S. Forces in Iraq," Congressional Research Service, July 24, 2008. http://fpc.state.gov.

by the French, Chinese, and Americans, among others and that, if they remained angry at all their invaders, they would have no friends.

During the waning weeks of World War II, meanwhile, military planners estimated that it might take 1,000,000 American casualties to invade and conquer the Japanese homeland. Instead, Pres. Harry Truman opted to drop the atomic bomb, killing 140,000 in Nagasaki and Hiroshima. Today, Japan is our closest ally and friend in the Far East, and has been for years.

The Middle East will be a difficult area in which to establish peace and democracy, which are not always one and the same. Most of the Middle East was part of the Ottoman sultanate, the last of the great Muslim empires. This empire was defeated during the World War I. Since England and France had won the war, the empire was divided and the Arabic-speaking provinces, the fertile crescent, were split into three new countries: Iraq and Palestine (under a British mandate) and Syria (under the French). The French then made a further division, creating Lebanon and Syria. Thereafter, the British divided Palestine on both sides of the River Jordan: Trans Jordan to the east and Palestine to the west. The Arabian Peninsula was inaccessible desert and its rulers were allowed to maintain their independence. The Turks freed their homeland through a secular nationalist movement led by Kemal Ataturk, who, in 1924, abolished the sultanate and adopted Western ways.

We complain about sectarian violence [in Iraq] but, as we review our own history, we find that fighting over issues of church and state were quite vicious in the West as well.

The Middle East and U.S. History

The outline of Western constitutional and democratic history provides clues as to why it may take some time for democratic instincts and practices to develop in Iraq. We complain about sectarian violence there but, as we review our own history, we find that fighting over issues of church and state were quite vicious in the West as well. Likewise, it took several centuries for England, France, and the U.S. to work out the details of their present forms of democracy. We complain about the Shiites and Sunnis engaging in civil war, but aren't we forgetting that the bloodiest conflict in American history was our own Civil War?

We must be more patient with the Iraqis, who grew up governed by a patriarchy of tribal leaders. Their instincts, honed by centuries of practice, are to distrust political decisions made by the new democratic government that has been formed. While patience may be asked of the American electorate, it does not appear to be forthcoming. Ultimately, a hastier withdrawal and a less-than-perfect political solution than originally was planned for may turn out to be the only way to extricate the nation from this quagmire.

The U.S. Military Presence in Iraq Is Essential for Iraqi Democracy

Steven Groves

In the following viewpoint, Steven Groves argues against a withdrawal of U.S. forces from Iraq. The author examines the range of programs that the United States has implemented in order to promote democracy and help build civil society in Iraq. He also explores the challenges that nongovernmental organizations (NGOs) face in the country. Finally, Groves details steps that should be taken to prevent the spread of Iraqi violence and instability. Steven Groves is the Bernard and Barbara Lomas Fellow at the Heritage Foundation and director of the organization's Freedom Project.

As you read, consider the following questions:

1. According to Groves, what efforts or projects have nongovernmental organizations undertaken since the end of U.S. combat operations?

2. What U.S. organization does Groves assert established the first free Iraqi news service and public broadcasting agency?

3. According to the viewpoint, what part of Iraqi society is most crucial to the building of a civil society and most likely to flee if violence expands in the country?

Steven Groves, "Advancing Freedom in Iraq," *Backgrounder*, no. 2056, July 30, 2007. www.heritage.org. Heritage Foundation. Reproduced by permission.

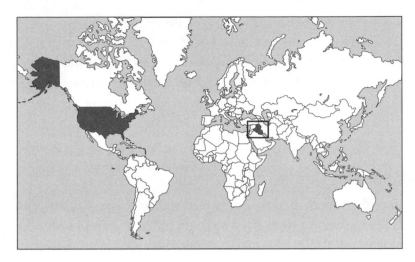

Helping Iraq to become a secure and stable nation in the heart of the Middle East is in the national interest of the United States. Iraq's best chance for long-term stability is to develop democratic institutions that will protect the basic civil, political, and human liberties and rights of the Iraqi people.

Non-governmental organizations dedicated to democracy promotion have been operating in Iraq since the fall of Baghdad in April 2003. Their activities include promoting civic participation in government, strengthening political parties, supporting the political participation of women, and promoting good governance.

In Iraq, freedom, democracy, and civil society—nonexistent under Saddam Hussein—remain precarious. U.S. government efforts, as well as the efforts of non-governmental organizations, to promote democracy and good governance rely on the security umbrella provided by the U.S. military presence. A precipitous U.S. military withdrawal would almost certainly doom U.S. and Iraqi efforts to build a free and democratic Iraq.

The Shiites, Sunnis, Kurds, and other factions require a secure environment to reach political accommodation. The United States and the international community should do everything possible to help to stabilize Iraq. Specifically, the U.S. Congress should not interfere with ongoing military efforts to secure and stabilize Iraq or legislate restrictions on the use of U.S. military force. . . .

Promoting Democracy in Iraq

Since the end of major combat operations, the United States has been working with Iraqi citizens to build democratic institutions and strengthen civil society through the U.S. Department of State, the U.S. Agency for International Development, and various non-governmental organizations (NGOs). These efforts include projects to strengthen human rights, political and civic participation, women's rights, religious tolerance, good governance, and anti-corruption efforts and to establish an independent media.

Democracy Promotion by U.S. NGOs. Non-governmental organizations dedicated to democracy promotion have been operating in Iraq since the fall of Baghdad in April 2003. Their activities include promoting civic participation in government, strengthening political parties, supporting the political participation of women, and promoting good governance.

These NGOs—including the National Endowment for Democracy and its major grantees: the National Democratic Institute for International Affairs (NDI), the International Republican Institute (IRI), and the Center for International Private Enterprise (CIPE)—work alongside Iraqi citizens to form and strengthen organizations that have become actively involved in Iraq's fledgling political process.

- The NDI and IRI host focus groups on a variety of political and public policy issues, facilitate regular meetings between Iraqi citizens and government officials, conduct national opinion polls, organize seminars to discuss the role of civil society organizations in a democracy, and arrange workshops to build the capacity of civic organizations to participate actively in the political process.

- CIPE concentrates on assisting Iraqi business leaders and other civil society groups in building a foundation for economic growth and democratic stability. Iraq's multitudinous political parties have received training in party organization, leadership, message development, voter outreach, communication, and media relations in an effort to build and strengthen political pluralism.

To date, approximately 8,000 national, regional, and local government officials have been trained in an effort to promote transparency, accountability, fiscal responsibility, and other means of engendering governmental integrity.

Upon arriving in Iraq, the NDI sought to reach out to as many Iraqis as possible. In addition to establishing a headquarters office in Baghdad outside the Green Zone, it set up branch resource offices in Basrah, Hillah, Tikrit, Kirkuk, and Irbil. The branch offices were staffed by U.S. and Iraqi personnel and equipped with meeting rooms, libraries, and computer facilities, which were made accessible to local Iraqis interested in improving their respective communities. The branch offices served approximately 3,500 Iraqis each month. The NDI also helped to set up the lower house of the Iraqi legislature, the Council of Representatives, by providing technical assistance and support in helping legislators to learn their roles and responsibilities in a democratic body.

U.S. Agency for International Development. U.S. government efforts to promote democracy, good governance, and individual rights are coordinated primarily through the U.S. Agency for International Development (USAID). For example, USAID initiated the Iraq Civil Society and Independent Media

Program to support the establishment of an "informed, sustainable, and active Iraqi civil society" that will participate in Iraq's nascent democracy.

As part of its efforts, USAID established four regional Civil Society Resource Centers in Baghdad, Irbil, Hillah, and Basrah, which coordinate services for all 18 Iraqi governorates. The resource centers are staffed by personnel from America's Development Foundation (a U.S. nonprofit organization) and local Iraqis who provide training, technical assistance, and grants for developing Iraqi civil society organizations (CSOs). The resource centers have hosted over 1,100 training workshops to develop the core capabilities of the Iraqi CSOs.

The Iraqi CSOs stood up by USAID focus their efforts on several areas, including combating corruption, which was endemic under Saddam. To date, approximately 8,000 national, regional, and local government officials have been trained in an effort to promote transparency, accountability, fiscal responsibility, and other means of engendering governmental integrity. USAID and the Iraqi CSOs foster human rights by training Iraqis to monitor, report, and document human rights abuses.

Free and independent media have flourished in Iraq since the fall of Baghdad. USAID's Iraq Civil Society and Independent Media Program "is the only substantial supporter of in-country training, technical assistance, and funding" to Iraq's media sector. Through these efforts, USAID successfully established the first independent Iraqi news agency and the first independent public broadcasting service in the Arab world.

Under Saddam's highly centralized regime, Iraqis had no say in the national government and participated little in local governance issues. Community Action Programs (CAPs), a USAID grassroots effort, are aimed at alleviating that deficit. USAID works through several partners to manage reconstruction programs throughout Iraq.

The CAPs are intended to engage the Iraqi populace directly in planning and implementing rehabilitation and reconstruction projects in their own communities, thereby educating Iraqis in the fundamentals of democracy. These local rehabilitation projects "encourage communities to organize and elect inclusive and representative neighborhood councils" that then operate in a transparent and accountable manner to identify and prioritize community needs and to complete the projects. These grassroots efforts are critical to developing a capacity for local governance where it did not exist before.

In the worst-case scenario, a Sunni-Shi'a civil war could spread beyond Iraq and become an international conflagration, engulfing Iraq's neighbors (and probably the U.S.) in a regional war.

USAID also operates in Iraq as part of multi-agency groups called Provincial Reconstruction Teams (PRTs). PRTs are relatively small operational units that are composed of U.S. diplomats, military officers, development policy specialists, and other stabilization experts. The military provides operational support and security for U.S. civilian personnel who work in PRTs, which are located in almost every province of Iraq.

The PRTs work with local Iraqi leaders to build local capacity in good governance, reconstruction, and economic development. Funding for reconstruction projects is provided through microloans and grants. Like the CAPs, the PRTs aim to train local Iraqi leaders in delivering essential services to their respective communities. To this end, the PRTs build relationships with local business and community leaders who desire to build a peaceful and democratic Iraq.

The Dangers of a U.S. Withdrawal

There are several dire predictions of what will happen in Iraq if the U.S. military withdraws. One possibility is that simmering sectarian violence would escalate into a full-scale Sunni-Shi'a civil war that would consume all of Iraq. Such an internecine civil war could topple the central government and its institutions and fragment the Iraqi armed forces. The steady stream of Iraqis leaving for Jordan, Egypt, and elsewhere could grow into a wholesale exodus. The resulting humanitarian crisis could lead to the deaths of hundreds of thousands of Iraqis. In the worst-case scenario, a Sunni-Shi'a civil war could spread beyond Iraq and become an international conflagration, engulfing Iraq's neighbors (and probably the U.S.) in a regional war.

The common thread of these predictions is that a U.S. troop withdrawal would lead to chaos throughout Iraq and that democracy, human rights, the rule of law, and individual freedoms would be among the first casualties. A complete breakdown of the Iraqi government would lead to anarchy and place Iraqi citizens in survival mode in which the safety and survival of their families would be more important than the advancement of democratic ideals.

Increasingly, members of Congress are calling for the United States to withdraw from Iraq. Congress has already passed legislation, which the President vetoed, that would have "redeployed" U.S. armed forces out of Iraq and restricted the use of U.S. troops to extremely limited circumstances, such as killing or capturing members of al Qaeda and training Iraqi security forces. Although this legislation stated that U.S. forces were permitted to provide protection for "American diplomatic facilities and American citizens" (such as the U.S. embassy and diplomatic personnel), it designated no specific facilities or citizens for protection. Neither did it provide any specific protection for USAID, NGOs such as the NDI and their Iraqi employees, or the Provincial Reconstruction Teams operating in Iraq.

Iraqi's 2005 Elections

"This is the greatest day in the history of this country," Iraqi national security adviser Mowaffak al-Rubaie told CNN. . . .

Insurgents had vowed to wash the streets with "voters' blood," and more than a dozen attacks killed at least 28 people and wounded 71 others.

But authorities said extensive security measures prevented more widespread car bombings and other attacks that many had feared would mar the elections.

"The streets of Baghdad were not filled with blood as the threats of terrorist groups had mentioned," election official Faryid Ayar said. "[Terrorists] directed a message to us: the message of killing. And we directed to them the message of elections and freedom and democracy."

Christiane Amanpour, Jane Arraf, Nic Robertson, Auday Sadeq, Ingrid Formanek and Mohammed Tawfeeq, "Sporadic Violence Doesn't Deter Iraqi Voters," January 31, 2005. www.cnn.com.

The ongoing effort of the U.S. government and NGOs to support the growth of Iraqi democracy would be an underappreciated victim of the anarchy that would follow a U.S. military withdrawal.

Democracy in Iraq Through NGOs

NGO efforts to promote democracy would very likely come to an abrupt end in the chaos that would follow a U.S. withdrawal. NGOs operating in Iraq already face considerable challenges due to the volatile security environment. Indeed, violence and gangsterism already have caused some prominent NGOs to close their operations in Iraq. For example, the Cooperative for Assistance and Relief Everywhere (CARE) terminated its operations in Iraq after Margaret Hassan, a naturalized Iraqi citizen working for CARE, was kidnapped and murdered in October 2004.

Democracy-promotion NGOs have also been affected by the violence. A fatal ambush on an NDI convoy in January 2007 obligated the NDI to close its resource centers in Basrah, Hillah, Tikrit, and Kirkuk and confine its operations to the relative safety of the Green Zone, Irbil (northern Iraq), and Amman, Jordan. The Irbil operation, which serves Iraqis living there and those who travel from Mosul and Kirkuk, will also become untenable if there is a significant U.S. military withdrawal.

The mere presence of NGOs provides a morale boost to the Iraqi people.

A major downturn in the security environment may make travel in the region too dangerous for the NDI to sustain its Irbil presence. NDI operations in the Green Zone are already suffering as a result of safety concerns caused by the shift of security responsibilities from the U.S. military to Iraqi forces.

Although the U.S. military does not provide physical security or force protection for NDI facilities, its presence provides a significant psychological assurance to NDI employees and the Iraqis who interact with the NDI. With the U.S. presence ensuring that Iraq will not slip into total anarchy, Iraqis are more likely to participate in programs that promote democracy and community governance.

The mere presence of NGOs provides a morale boost to the Iraqi people. For example, the closure of the NDI's Tikrit office prompted a great community outpouring. The NDI received hundreds of letters from the citizens of Tikrit imploring it not to close the office. The NGO operations also show the Iraqi people that other people in the world care about their well-being and hope that their situation will improve.

A significant drawdown of U.S. forces would also likely degrade security on the roads linking Iraq's airports to the major city centers where the democracy-promotion NGOs operate. For example, if the roads to the airports were not safe to travel, NDI employees would find maintaining operations in the Green Zone and Irbil to be difficult if not impossible. Travel between the NDI's office in Amman, Jordan, and other offices in Iraq would also be seriously compromised.

USAID Organizations Rely on the U.S. Military

If the U.S. military withdrew, USAID's efforts to promote democracy in Iraq would fare no better than the NGO activities. USAID's Civil Society Resource Centers and Community Action Programs operate "outside the wire" and therefore rely on the U.S. military presence to provide a security umbrella.

The Civil Society Resource Centers and the CAPs are not protected by the U.S. military, but U.S. forces are generally available if USAID personnel are attacked. For example, U.S. forces have the capability to send a quick-reaction force to aid USAID convoys if they should come under attack. The military can also provide emergency medical evacuations for any casualties.

The rise in sectarian violence and general chaos that would likely follow a significant U.S. military drawdown would inevitably lead to additional middle-class flight. At present, a strong U.S. presence provides the Iraqi people with the assurance that Iraq will not devolve into total anarchy.

However, a complete U.S. military withdrawal or even a withdrawal that leaves reduced forces behind for counterterrorism missions would eliminate the possibility of medical evacuations and rescues by quick-reaction forces. Furthermore, the resulting decline in general security would likely force the closure of the resource centers in Irbil, Hillah, and Basrah.

Similarly, the Provincial Reconstruction Teams spread across Iraq would likely cease operations if their military components were withdrawn. The security situation at the PRTs would be untenable without the operational security and support provided by U.S. forces. For example, there is no PRT in Najaf province because U.S. forces withdrew from that province in May 2004. If U.S. forces were withdrawn from the PRT operations in other provinces (e.g., Ninawa, Kirkuk, Diyala, and Anbar), the diplomatic and economic components of the PRTs probably could not continue their democratization and stabilization efforts.

Middle-Class Flight

The general chaos caused by a significant withdrawal of U.S. forces would likely exacerbate the current trend of Iraq's middle class fleeing the country. Involving the middle class is crucial to democracy building in Iraq. Civil society organizations draw their membership from the middle class, which is generally more educated and politically active than lower socioeconomic groups. If accelerated by an outbreak of anarchy, the middle-class "brain drain" could be a fatal blow to efforts to promote freedom and democracy in Iraq.

Iraq's middle class, which was greatly harmed under Saddam, has been leaving in steadily increasing numbers over the past several years. The United Nations estimates that roughly 40 percent of Iraq's middle class has left since 2003. Due to the current instability in Iraq, many of the Iraqis who once worked with the NDI have left for Jordan, Canada, and Australia, and most of the Iraqis currently working with the NDI aspire to follow their countrymen out of Iraq.

One of the primary reasons for middle-class flight is the deteriorating security environment caused by widespread sectarian violence, which escalated after the February 2006 bombing of the Shiite Askariya shrine in Samarra. In addition, gangster militiamen such as those employed by Moqtada al-Sadr have infiltrated and taken over the operation of schools, government ministries, and businesses. The resulting random violence and intimidation have further accelerated the departure of Iraq's teachers, civil servants, and business owners.

The rise in sectarian violence and general chaos that would likely follow a significant U.S. military drawdown would inevitably lead to additional middle-class flight. At present, a strong U.S. presence provides the Iraqi people with the assurance that Iraq will not devolve into total anarchy. If middle-class Iraqis lose that assurance, they will likely join their fellow refugees in Jordan, Syria, and other countries in the Middle East and Europe. Once gone and settled elsewhere, these Iraqis will likely never return.

What Should Be Done

The United States and the international community should do everything within their power to stabilize Iraq and to secure an environment in which Iraq's political factions can reach an accommodation. Only then can democracy grow and thrive where it has never existed before. Specifically, the United States should:

Give the "surge" time to succeed. A stable and secure Iraq where a fair and free democracy can thrive will not exist until the various Iraqi factions reach a final political reconciliation. The purpose of the "surge strategy" is to create just such an environment. U.S. troops for the surge finished arriving in mid-June [2007], when major military operations began. The results will not be clear for many months, but many armchair generals are already rushing to declare defeat. U.S. forces should be permitted to complete their mission of securing

Baghdad and degrading the capabilities of foreign fighters and "insurgents" who are seeking to destabilize Iraq.

Not impose any legislative restrictions on U.S. military missions. U.S. forces currently can intervene anywhere in Iraq, thereby providing both direct and indirect security for democracy-promotion efforts. Congressional legislation restricting the military to training the Iraqi forces and performing counterterrorism missions against al Qaeda would fail to provide the security environment necessary for the U.S. government and the NGO community to promote democracy, good governance, human rights, and the rule of law throughout Iraq. Without such protection, the operations of democracy-promotion NGOs, USAID, Provincial Reconstruction Teams, and Community Action Programs and other efforts to build and nurture Iraq's civil society would be jeopardized.

Secure the Green Zone. The Green Zone—once a safe haven for the Iraqi government, democracy-promotion NGOs, and other NGOs operating in Baghdad—has become increasingly dangerous since security responsibilities were partially transferred to Iraqi forces. The U.S. should recommit itself to providing force protection to the Green Zone so that the Iraqi government and the NGO community can continue to operate in relative security.

Continue to fund and support democracy promotion. Congress should continue to fund the efforts of the Department of State, USAID, the National Endowment for Democracy, the National Democratic Institute, the International Republican Institute, the Center for International Private Enterprise, and other NGOs operating in Iraq. The United States should encourage other U.N. [United Nations] member states to contribute or increase their contributions to the U.N. Democracy Fund, which has the mission of promoting democracy and strengthening civil society in Iraq and other countries that are making the transition to democracy around the world. U.N. Democracy Fund projects in Iraq include efforts to build an independent national news agency, strengthen local governance, and facilitate human rights seminars and workshops.

Why the U.S. Should Stay

There are many compelling reasons why the United States should not precipitously withdraw its military from Iraq. The general chaos and anarchy that would likely result from a U.S. military withdrawal could lead to the collapse of Iraq's government, dissolution of Iraqi armed forces, a refugee and humanitarian crisis, a middle-class exodus, and—in the worst-case scenario—a regional conflagration that would require renewed U.S. military intervention in even greater numbers.

A precipitous troop withdrawal would also be a disastrous setback in the war against terrorism. Such a retreat would weaken efforts to contain Iran and likely destabilize the Middle East well beyond Iraq's borders. It would undermine not only U.S. national interests, but also American ideals, such as freedom and democracy.

The United States has a responsibility to leave an Iraq that is in better condition than it was in when Saddam's regime was toppled. Iraqis must be given a chance to build a stable, secure nation that respects its own citizens and does not threaten its neighbors. Only a free and democratic Iraq will become a long-term military ally and economic partner for the United States.

USAID personnel and democracy-promotion NGOs are risking their lives to promote good governance, the rule of law, and human rights in offices and military bases located throughout Iraq. U.S. forces should be permitted to provide the security umbrella necessary for these efforts to succeed. Abandoning the Iraqis in their time of need would condemn them to a life of chaos and could spawn another Saddam-type authoritarian government—or worse.

Iraq's Ongoing Civil Strife Is a Struggle Between Democracy and Dictatorship

Howar Ziad

In the following viewpoint, Howar Ziad details the historical and philosophical reasons why Iraq has faced challenges in its effort to democratize. Ziad specifically accuses the supporters of the former regime of Saddam Hussein, known as Baathist, and their al Qaeda allies of waging a campaign against democracy and representative government. Ziad also stresses the importance of a democratic Iraq to the region and to the international community. Ziad is a former representative to the United Nations and currently the Iraqi ambassador to Canada.

As you read, consider the following questions:

1. How long did Saddam Hussein's Baathist Party rule Iraq?
2. According to the viewpoint, what percentage of Iraqis was represented by the government as of 2006?
3. What group in Iraq was the target of the 1988 genocide?

A s Iraqis are discovering, politics in a democracy is an indefinite business. The great English philosopher Michael Oakeshott said that in a democracy, "men sail a boundless and

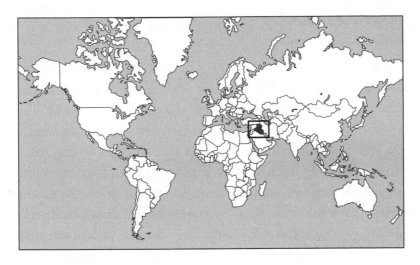

bottomless sea." A legitimate election—the basis of liberal democracy—is always elusive to forecasts and prediction. Public
opinion changes, and what was fashionable yesterday is politically poisonous today. Democracy is especially uncertain for
those in power, the politicians themselves. By contrast, dictatorships offer certainty for politicians. Even if they hold elections, the results are known in advance. As long as they hold
all but themselves in fear, their futures are fixed, and their political activity faces no genuine censure.

Challenges to Democracy in Iraq

The contrast between democracy and dictatorship explains
much of what is happening in Iraq. Diehard fascists, the rem-
nants of Saddam Hussein's regime and al Qaeda fanatics, have
waged a relentless campaign against the Iraqi people. They
have allowed Iraqi citizens almost no rest, no opportunity to
heal the wounds of 35 years of Baathist [the Party of Saddam
Hussein and the Sunnis] totalitarianism. This faction, which
subscribes to the dark days of state brutality in Iraqi history,
has viciously attacked schoolchildren, mosques, churches, fu-
nerals, and hospitals. They provoke murderous sectarianism in
an attempt to undo every weave of the country's social fabric.

Outrageously, foreign apologists dress up their ruthless acts of murder as a so-called "national resistance."

Despite the violent challenges that we face from fanatics in our attempt to establish a secure and stable democratic state, our aim is to go further than mere democracy and to build an Iraqi national consensus. The majority of Iraqis has insisted on a principle of inclusiveness over one of narrow majoritarianism. We have already built a government that represents over 80 per cent of Iraqis, and now we are trying to accommodate the remainder. Most members of the Sunni Arab community of Iraq reject terrorism; it is only a violent minority that wishes to wreck a peaceful and democratic future.

The stakes in Iraq are enormous. This should activate our resolve and impel us to comprehend how important it is that we fight for democracy in Iraq to our last breath.

By building a political consensus that empowers the decent and lawful majority, we give ourselves the best chance to defeat the fascist threat to Iraq. We must accept that it is possible to lose Iraq to Saddamism and jihadism, and imagine the horrific consequences of such a defeat.

The stakes in Iraq are enormous. This should activate our resolve and impel us to comprehend how important it is that we fight for democracy in Iraq to our last breath. We must, as Winston Churchill would have said, fight them in the streets, in the roads, in the villages and in the countryside.

The problem is that building a consensus takes time, which is why we do not have a government yet [as of Spring 2006] in Iraq following the Dec. 15, 2005, elections. The lengthy debate over the office of prime minister underscores the fact that leaders will be held accountable in the new Iraq, and that these matters will be subject to deliberation. It is, however, wrong to say that there is no government in Iraq today. The

Iraq's Political Progress

On the political front, Iraq has seen bottom-up progress. Tribes and other groups in the provinces who fought terror are now turning to rebuilding local political structures and taking charge of their own affairs. Progress in the provinces is leading to progress in Baghdad, as Iraqi leaders increasingly act together, share power, and forge compromises on behalf of the nation. Upcoming elections will consolidate this progress and provide a way for Iraqis to settle disputes through the political process instead of through violence. Iraqis plan to hold provincial elections later this year, and these will be followed by national elections in 2009.

Iraq will increase its engagement in the world and the world must increase its engagement with Iraq. A stable, successful, and independent Iraq is in the strategic interests of Arab nations and all who want peace in the Middle East, and we will urge them to increase their support this year.

The White House, "Fact Sheet: The Way Forward in Iraq,"
April 10, 2008. www.whitehouse.gov.

government selected by parliament following Iraq's first democratic elections in January of 2005 continues to serve.

Consensus matters to the new Iraq because it is a fundamental rejection of modern Iraqi history. A failed state since its inception in 1921, Iraq was, at best, run by an unrepresentative clique and, more recently, by the whim of one man with the occasional input of his psychopathic sons. Saddam Hussein and the Baath Party refined criminality. They used ethnic cleansing and mass murder as tools of statecraft, making Baathism a form of domestic colonialism. Iraqi Kurdistan was colonized systematically with Arab settlers (a process that the Iraqi monarchy had started). Ethnic cleansing was systematic and part of the function of the state. The genocide of the Kurds in the 1988 Anfal campaign (including the gassing of Halabja) was not an aberration but a logical consequence of the Sunni Arab supremacist-nationalist ideology that has cursed the peace of the Middle East. Genocide was also practised against Iraq's Shia Arabs in the historic marshlands while, in the cities, the Baathists aimed to leave the Shia Arab community leaderless and reduce it to a second-class population.

The Need for International Assistance

The feeble international reaction to these crimes remains a matter of great bitterness to Iraqis, who paid a heavy price in blood for the politics of so-called "stability."

It is this bitter history, coupled with the willingness of most Iraqis to seek reconciliation and not revenge, that makes our political process move at a slower pace than many would like. To achieve peace, Iraqis need to be autonomous and united, which is why Iraq now has a federal constitution built on the principle of extensive self-government for Iraq's different regional communities.

Canadians, experienced in dynamics of a united federation, can set the example for the international community, by assisting the Iraqi people as they move along their federal path.

Iraqis refuse to allow their history to be their prison. They reject the notion that the Middle East cannot be democratic because it does not have the right culture; indeed, they reject this idea every day when they overwhelmingly reject revenge and, instead, seek reconciliation.

Their democratically elected representatives may be slow to decide, but their deliberations are peaceful and reasoned. It is they, the democratically chosen leaders of the new Iraq, who represent the true spirit of the country, not the violent minority who have chosen fascism and violence.

Iraq Needs an Authoritarian Regime, Not a Democracy

Yossi Alpher

In the following viewpoint, Yossi Alpher advances the idea that the best policy for the United States in Iraq is to install an authoritarian government. He contends that the effort to create a democracy in Iraq has been an utter failure and has contributed to regional instability. Alpher points out that most of the other major allies of the United States in the region are not democracies and that the best chance for political liberalization will occur under an authoritarian regime. Yossi Alpher is a former senior advisor to the Israeli government and the editor of an online publishing company.

As you read, consider the following questions:

1. According to the viewpoint, what has happened to the American government's thesis about the democratization of Iraq?
2. What does Alpher claim would be the result in the region if the United States withdrew its military forces from Iraq?
3. What does the author assert is the only strategy to overcome the "regional damage" done by the U.S.-led war?

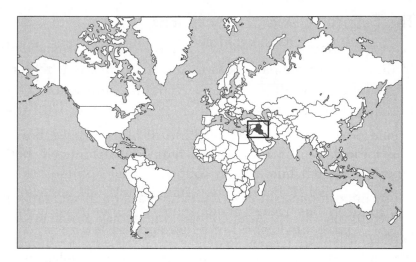

The only sacred cow left to slaughter in Iraq is the illusion that somehow, if the United States persists, democracy will survive and reign, and be good for America and its interests. Admitting that democratization has failed and abandoning the democratization project is the real issue still to be confronted in the course of extricating the United States from Iraq without leaving behind total regional disaster.

All the other excuses for occupying Iraq have long been discarded. No weapons of mass destruction were found. There is far more terrorism there now than under Saddam Hussein. Direct American access to Middle East oil has only contributed to driving up the price. Charter members of the "axis of evil" are now candidates for compromise agreements with the United States.

Anyone who thought getting rid of Saddam was good for Israel now has to contend in Iraq with Sunni jihadis, pro-Iranian Shias and the Iranians themselves. Even the thesis that democratization of Iraq would somehow radiate to surrounding countries has been dropped: the [George W.] Bush administration has stopped pressuring autocracies like Egypt to democratize and is trying to undo the consequences of Palestinian democratization.

The Failure of Democracy in Iraq

Yet, the "democratic" regime Washington installed in Baghdad in the course of the past four years is still in place. It reflects the unique brand of American exceptionalism espoused by President Bush and the neoconservatives, together with the president's evangelical belief that the evils of Islamist terror can be vanquished by means of a healthy dose of "liberty" and other American values.

By imposing instant electoral democracy on a traumatized and ethnically divided Arab country and allowing militant Islamists with their militias to run in and win elections there, the United States has created a dysfunctional and violent polity. As matters now stand, once American forces go home Iraq will quickly become a fragmented and divisive state or states—part or all of which are dominated by Iran—that draws Iraq's neighbors into ethnic and religious conflict.

The present American-designed regime will not survive without the United States Army and Marines. The outcome for the region will be, quite simply, disaster. Stability in countries like Jordan and Kuwait will be seriously threatened. Iran's long arm will intimidate the region. Israel's security situation will worsen perceptibly.

The stakes, then, are huge. Hence, the United States must not only try to restore a semblance of order before it withdraws. It must find a way to dismantle the grotesque parody of democracy it has created in Iraq.

The U.S. Must Install an Authoritarian Regime in Iraq

Because the implantation of genuine democracy is impossible for Washington under present circumstances—and bearing in mind that Iraq with its history of violence and divisive sectarian composition is probably the last, rather than the first, Arab state in which such an experiment should have been car-

Even Republicans Doubt the Utility of Democracy in Iraq

The Bush administration is facing fresh doubts from some Republicans who say its emphasis on promoting democracy around the world has come at the expense of protecting other American interests.

The second thoughts signify a striking change in mood over one of President Bush's cherished tenets, pitting Republicans who call themselves realists against the neoconservatives who saw the invasion of Iraq as a catalyst for change and who remain the most vigorous advocates of a muscular American campaign to foster democratic movements.

"You are hearing more and more questions about the administration's approach on this issue," said Lorne W. Craner, president of the International Republican Institute.... "The 'realists' in the party are rearing their heads and asking, 'Is this stuff working?'"

Steven Weisman,
"Democracy Push by Bush Attracts Doubters in Party,"
New York Times, *March 17, 2006. www.nytimes.com.*

ried out in the first place—America must now seek to leave behind a friendly authoritarian regime.

This is clearly a very politically incorrect idea, even for Americans and others in the democratic West who oppose the American presence and want it to end quickly. Nor is it easy for an Israeli who enjoys the fruits of democracy to make this proposal.

I apologize to my liberal friends and acquaintances in the Arab world who have struggled so hard for democratic progress and who welcomed the Bush administration's attempt to impose democracy. Even they must recognize that that attempt not only failed, but was seriously counterproductive, particularly in Iraq and Palestine. Even they must concede that the way to democratize Arab countries is from within.

Dismantling Iraq's democracy-cum-militia rule provides the only hope for genuinely reducing the regional damage wreaked by the American misadventure in Iraq. Quite simply, a way has to be found to declare martial law—heaven knows there are plenty of reasons to do that in Iraq—and install an emergency regime.

Undoing some of the damage in Iraq, so as to block Iranian hegemonic expansion westward and thwart Islamic militants, is far more important for the United States and the Middle East . . . than persisting with a failed and destructive experiment in democratization.

Bush's spinmasters can always soften the blow to the president's prestige by describing the new order in palatable quasi-democratic terms, as long as that order is predominantly Shia, pro-Western, very tough and not tainted by pro-Iranian and pro-Islamist figures and sentiments.

This is what all of Iraq's neighbors, save the Iranians, want. Of course, there is no guarantee that such a regime would survive. But it gives Iraq and the region a better chance to emerge from the transition engendered by America's eventual departure with Iraq remaining in one piece and not under Iranian, or in the case of Anbar province, militant Sunni, domination.

Perhaps sometime soon, a smarter, more patient and more sensitive American government can again try to foster and encourage democracy in the Middle East. Certainly it can be sensitive to the need to pressure Arab dictatorships to liberalize.

But gradually: America's allies in the region are nearly all autocrats, not democrats. More important, Israel's partners in peace in the Arab world, Egypt and Jordan, are autocratic regimes, not democratic ones like Hamas in Palestine. So much for the theories of Natan Sharanasky and Benjamin Netanyahu about Israel being able to make peace only with democracies.

The strategic bottom line is clear: Undoing some of the damage in Iraq, so as to block Iranian hegemonic expansion westward and thwart Islamist militants, is far more important for the United States and the Middle East at this juncture in time than persisting with a failed and destructive experiment in democratization.

Periodical Bibliography

The following articles have been selected to supplement the diverse views presented in this chapter.

Eva Bellin   "Democracy and Its Discontents," *Foreign Affairs*, July/August, 2008.

Stephen Biddle   "Defining Victory and Defeat in Iraq," *National Interest*, November/December, 2006.

William Buckley   "How Long, How Long?" *National Review*, April 19, 2004.

Tom Engelhardt   "Iraq: The View from Year Six," *The Nation*, March 19, 2008.

Melvin Goodman   "Has the War in Iraq Helped to Spread Democracy?" *CQ Researcher*, April 2005.

Lawrence Kaplan   "Aim Low," *The New Republic*, November 7, 2005.

Charles Krauthammer   "Why It Deserves the Hype," *Time*, February 14, 2005.

Naim Moises   "Casualties of War," *Foreign Policy*, September/October 2004.

Tom Rockmore   "Can War Transform Iraq into a Democracy?" *Theoria: A Journal of Social and Political Theory*, April 2004.

Y. Satanovsky   "A Five-Year War for Oil and Democracy," *International Affairs*, Fall 2008.

Roger Scott   "Imperialist Democracy, Ancient Athenians and the US Presence in Iraq," *Australian Journal of International Affairs*, September 2005.

Fareed Zakaria   "Elections Are Not Democracy," *Newsweek*, February 7, 2008.

For Further Discussion

Chapter 1

1. Amir Taheri outlines the main reasons behind France's opposition to the Iraq War, including the relationship between French President Jacques Chirac and Iraqi leader Saddam Hussein. Does he make a strong case that French policies were based on personal interaction? Are his arguments credible?

2. Suzanne Maloney contends that the U.S.-led invasion of Iraq has strengthened the standing of Iran in the region. What were the major mistakes made by the United States? Could they have been avoided?

3. According to the viewpoint by Frank Laybourn, what were the main reasons that Denmark supported the U.S.-led invasion of Iraq? How important was U.S.-Danish solidarity in the decision to back the war?

Chapter 2

1. According to the viewpoint by Justin Vaisse, what are the main areas of convergence between U.S. and French foreign policy toward the Middle East? What are the main areas of divergence?

2. Colin Rubenstein is very critical of suggestions that the United States expand its diplomatic efforts concerning ending the Iraq War to include Iran. Does the author make a good argument? What are the main weaknesses of the viewpoint?

3. According to Dore Gold, Iraq did not pose a significant threat to Israel or to regional stability. What countries does Gold argue were a more serious threat? Why does the author argue that people link the Iraq conflict with Israel?

Chapter 3

1. Rod Liddle questions the links between the Iraq War and terrorism in the United Kingdom. According to his viewpoint, what are the main reasons for Islamic terrorism in the United Kingdom? What are the main flaws in his argument? What are the main strengths?

2. Reuel Marc Gerecht is a researcher at the conservative American Enterprise Institute. Does this association seem to influence his viewpoint? Or are his arguments fair and balanced?

3. Neil Mackay contends that the Iraq War has led to an increase in terrorism in countries such as Afghanistan and Pakistan. What are the main points that Mackay cites to support his arguments?

Chapter 4

1. David Wearing asserts that the United Kingdom made a number of mistakes during its occupation of southern Iraq. What does Wearing cite as the key errors? Could they have been avoided?

2. According to the viewpoint by Harold E. Rogers Jr., what were the main obstacles that the United States and its allies faced in their efforts to democratize Iraq and the broader Middle East? Why does the author advise patience on the part of the West in supporting democracy in Iraq?

3. What type of government in Iraq does Yossi Alpher argue would be best for regional peace and stability. Do you agree with his main points? Why or why not?

Organizations to Contact

American Enterprise Institute (AEI)
1150 Seventeenth Street NW, Washington, DC   20036
(202) 862-5800 • Fax: (202) 862-7177
E-mail: NRI@aei.org
Web site: www.AEI.org

The American Enterprise Institute (AEI) is a nonprofit, non-partisan research organization that was founded in 1943. The conservative AEI promotes limited government and advocates private-enterprise answers to public policy issues. The AEI generally supports a continued U.S. involvement in Iraq until a stable, democratic government is in place.

Brookings Institution
1775 Massachusetts Avenue NW, Washington, DC   20036
(202) 797 6000 • Fax: (202) 536 3623
E-mail: communications@brookings.edu
Web site: www.brookings.edu

The Brookings Institution was founded in 1927 and is one of the nation's most prominent nonprofit, nonpartisan research centers. It conducts research on both domestic and international issues, including foreign and security policy issues such as the Iraq War. The Brookings Institution has been critical of the Iraq War and the Bush administration's management of the conflict.

Canadian International Council (CIC)
45 Willcocks Street, Box 210, Toronto, Ontario   M5S 1C7
   Canada
Web site: www.igloo.org

The Canadian International Council (CIC) is a private, non-partisan institution devoted to research and the dissemination of knowledge on international affairs. The CIC works to bring together academics, public officials, and business leaders to discuss and debate foreign policy, including issues such as the Iraq War. The CIC produces a number of publications, including the prominent *International Journal*, founded in 1946.

Carnegie Endowment for International Peace

1779 Massachusetts Avenue NW, Washington, DC   20036
(202) 483 7600 • Fax: (202) 483 1840
E-mail: info@ceip.org
Web site: www.carnegieendowment.org

The Carnegie Endowment for International Peace was founded in 1910 to support international peace and stability. It is an independent, nonprofit research organization that sponsors studies on international security and globalization. Carnegie has produced a range of publications, studies, and other research on the causes of the Iraq War and its impact on world politics. The endowment publishes the prominent journal *Foreign Policy*.

Cato Institute

1000 Massachusetts Avenue NW, Washington, DC   20001
(202) 842-0200 • Fax: (202) 842 3490
E-mail: pr@cato.org
Web site: www.cato.org

The Cato Institute is an American nonprofit, libertarian research body. Cato was founded in 1977 by Edward H. Crane. The institute advocates for individual choice in public policy matters and limited government. It conducts a range of seminars and conferences and publishes a variety of research materials on government policy. It has produced materials both supportive and critical of the Iraq War and the Bush administration's management of the conflict.

Center for Independent Studies (CIS)

PO Box 92, St Leonards NSW   1590
   Australia
Phone: 61 2 9438 4377 • Fax: 61 2 9439 7310

E-mail: cis@cis.org.au
Web site: www.cis.org.au/

With offices in Australia and New Zealand, the Center for Independent Studies (CIS) is a nonprofit research organization that was founded in 1976. CIS endeavors to facilitate interaction between academics and policy makers on important issues to Australia and the broader Pacific region. It publishes a range of general studies, as well as commissioned studies on individual topics. CIS has generally been critical of the Iraq War and the subsequent U.S.-led occupation of Iraq.

Center for Strategic and International Studies (CSIS)
1800 K Street NW, Washington, DC   20006
(202) 887-0200 • Fax: (202) 775-3199
E-mail: aschwartz@csis.org
Web site: www.csis.org

The Center for Strategic and International Studies (CSIS) was founded in 1962 to provide cutting-edge research on international issues. CSIS is a nonprofit, nonpartisan research body that is currently one of the world's largest and most comprehensive policy think tanks. Its programs and researchers address all areas of global politics, including the Iraq War. CSIS publishes the influential journal *Washington Quarterly*.

Council on Foreign Relations (CFR)
1779 Massachusetts Avenue NW, Washington, DC   20036
(202) 483-7600 • Fax: (202) 483-1840
E-mail: info@cfr.org
Web site: www.cfr.org

The Council on Foreign Relations (CFR) was formed in 1921. CFR is a nonpartisan, nonprofit research organization. Its mission is to be a resource on foreign policy issues for business, government, and the public. CFR produces a range of reports, studies, and books. It also publishes the journal *Foreign Affairs*.

German Council on Foreign Relations (GCFR)
Berlin D-10787
  Germany
49(0)30 25 42 31-0 • Fax: 49(0)30 25 42 31-16
E-mail: info@dgap.org
Web site (English version): http://en.dgap.org/

The German Council on Foreign Relations (GCFR) is Germany's premier think tank on foreign policy and international relations. It is an independent, nonprofit research body that seeks to contribute to the policy-making process in Germany and to promote Germany's role in the world. The GCFR produces a number of publications on international security, in both English and German.

International Institute for Strategic Studies (IISS)
Arundel House, London WC2R 3DX
  United Kingdom
44 (0) 20 7379 7676 • Fax: 44 (0) 20 7836 3108
Web site: www.iiss.org

The International Institute for Strategic Studies (IISS) is a nonprofit British institute devoted to the study of international relations and global security. Founded in 1958, the IISS initially focused on nuclear deterrence. Currently it addresses the full range of economic, political, and security issues throughout the world. It has more than 2,500 members in more than 100 countries. IISS publishes a highly influential research series, the *Adelphi Papers*.

Royal United Service Institute (RUSI)
Whitehall, London SW1A 2ET Great Britain
  United Kingdom
44 (0)20 7930 5854
E-mail: daniels@rusi.org
Web site: www.rusi.org

The Royal United Service Institute (RUSI) is a renowned British organization that studies military policy and international security. RUSI was founded in 1831 by the Duke of Wellington to provide research on military issues. Today it conducts a range of activities but continues to concentrate on three core areas: international security, homeland security, and military science. It has produced a number of studies and publications on the Iraq War, in addition to bringing together world leaders and military officers to discuss the conflict in seminars and conferences.

Stockholm International Peace Research Institute (SIPRI)
Signalistgatan 9, Solna   SE-169 70
  Sweden
46-8-655-97-00 • Fax: 46-8-655-97-33
E-mail: sipri@sipri.org
Web site: www.sipri.org

The Stockholm International Peace Research Institute (SIPRI) is an independent research center that specializes in international peace and security issues. SIPRI publishes several annual reports on arms control and international conflict.

Bibliography of Books

John Agresto — *Mugged by Reality: The Liberation of Iraq and the Failure of Good Intentions.* New York: Encounter Books, 2007.

Christian Alfonsi — *Circle in the Sand: Why We Went Back to Iraq.* New York: Doubleday, 2006.

Daniel Benjamin and Stephan Simon — *The Next Attack: The Failure of the War on Terror and a Strategy for Getting It Right.* New York: Henry Holt, 2005.

Markus E. Bouillon, David M. Malone and Ben Rowswell — *Iraq: Preventing a New Generation of Conflict.* Boulder, CO: Lynne Rienner Publishers, 2007.

Joseph Braude — *The New Iraq: Rebuilding the Country, Its People, the Middle East and the World.* New York: Basic Books, 2003.

L. Paul Bremmer and Malcolm McConnell — *My Year in Iraq: The Struggle to Build a Future of Hope.* New York: Simon & Schuster, 2006.

Mary Buckley and Robert Singh, eds. — *The Bush Doctrine and the War on Terrorism: Global Responses, Global Consequences.* New York: Routledge, 2006.

Daniel L. Byman and Kenneth M. Pollack
Things Fall Apart: Containing the Spillover from an Iraqi Civil War. Washington, DC: Brookings Institution Press, 2007.

Jonathan Cook
Israel and the Clash of Civilizations: Iraq, Iran and the Plan to Remake the Middle East. Ann Arbor, MI: Pluto Press, 2008.

Ivo H. Daalder and James M. Lindsey
America Unbound: The Bush Revolution in Foreign Policy. Washington, DC: Brookings Institution Press, 2003.

James Fallows
Blind into Baghdad: America's War in Iraq. New York: Vintage Books, 2006.

Rick Fawn and Raymond Hinnebusch, eds.
The Iraq War: Causes and Consequences. Boulder, CO: Lynne Rienner Publishers, 2006.

Andrew Fiala
The Just War Myth: The Moral Illusions of War. Lanham, MD: Rowman and Littlefield, 2008.

David Frum
The Right Man: The Surprise Presidency of George W. Bush. Waterville, ME: Thorndyke Press, 2003.

David Frum and Richard Perle
An End to Evil: How to Win the War on Terror. New York: Random House, 2003.

Melvin A. Goodman
Failure of Intelligence: The Decline and Fall of the CIA. Lanham, MD: Rowman and Littlefield, 2008.

Mel Gurtov

Superpower on Crusade: The Bush Doctrine in US Foreign Policy. Boulder, CO: Lynne Rienner Publishers, 2006.

William Hale

Turkey, the US and Iraq. London, UK: London Middle East Institute, 2007.

Dale R. Herspring

Rumsfeld's Wars: The Arrogance of Power. Lawrence, KS: University Press of Kansas, 2008.

Robert Jervis

American Foreign Policy in a New Era. New York: Routledge, 2005.

Lawrence Kaplan and William Kristol

The War over Iraq: Saddam's Tyranny and America's Mission. San Francisco, CA: Encounter Books, 2003.

Sarwar Kashmeri

America and Europe After 9/11 and Iraq: The Great Divide. Westport, CT: Praeger, 2007.

Charles W. Kegley and Gregory A. Raymond

After Iraq: The Imperiled American Imperium. New York: Oxford University Press, 2007.

Stephen Kinzer

Overthrow: America's Century of Regime Change From Hawaii to Iraq. New York: Times Books, 2006.

James Mann

The Rise of the Vulcans: The History of Bush's War Cabinet. New York: Viking Penguin, 2004.

Alexander Moens

The Foreign Policy of George W. Bush: Values, Strategy and Loyalty. Aldershot, UK: Ashgate, 2004.

Heraldo Munoz — *A Solitary War: A Diplomat's Chronicle of the Iraq War and Its Lessons.* Golden, CO: Fulcrum, 2008.

Vittorio Emanuele Parsi — *The Inevitable Alliance: Europe and the United States Beyond Iraq.* New York: Palgrave Macmillan, 2006.

Robert J. Pauly and Tom Lansford — *Strategic Preemption: US Foreign Policy and the Second Iraq War.* Aldershot, UK: Ashgate Publishing, 2004.

Stephen C. Pelletiere — *Losing Iraq: Insurgency and Politics.* Westport, CT: Praeger, 2007.

Miriam Pemberton and William D. Hartung, eds. — *Lessons from Iraq: Avoiding the Next War.* Boulder, CO: Paradigm Publishers, 2008.

Kenneth M. Pollack — *The Threatening Storm: The Case for Invading Iraq.* New York: Random House, 2002.

Paul Rogers — *A War Too Far: Iraq, Iran and the New American Century.* Ann Arbor, MI: Pluto Press, 2006.

Barry Rubin — *The Long War for Freedom: The Arab Struggle for Democracy in the Middle East.* Hoboken, NJ: John Wiley & Sons, 2006.

David Ryan — *Frustrated Empire: US Foreign Policy 9/11 to Iraq.* Ann Arbor, MI: Pluto Press, 2007.

Ofira Seliktar   *The Politics of Intelligence and American Wars with Iraq.* New York: Palgrave Macmillan, 2008.

Simon Serfaty   *Architects of Delusion: Europe, America and the Iraq War.* Philadelphia, PA: University of Pennsylvania Press, 2008.

William Shawcross   *Allies: The U.S., Britain, Europe and the War in Iraq.* New York: Public Affairs, 2004.

Donald Snow   *What After Iraq?* New York: Pearson Longman, 2009.

Joseph E. Stiglitz and Linda J. Bilmes   *The Three Trillion Dollar War: The True Cost of the Iraq Conflict.* New York: W.W. Norton, 2008.

David Styan   *France & Iraq: Oil, Arms and French Policy Making in the Middle East.* New York: St. Martin's 2006.

Bing West   *The Strongest Tribe: War, Politics, and the Endgame in Iraq.* New York: Random House, 2008.

Bob Woodward   *Plan of Attack.* New York: Simon and Schuster, 2004.

Index

Geographic headings and page numbers in **boldface** refer to viewpoints about that country or region.